THE CONSCRIPTION OF FASHION

For Joan and Catherine and Oliver

THE CONSCRIPTION OF FASHION

Utility Cloth, Clothing and Footwear
1941–1952

Christopher Sladen

Published by
SCOLAR PRESS
Gower House
Croft Road
Aldershot
Hants GU11 3HR
England

Ashgate Publishing Company
Old Post Road
Brookfield
Vermont 05036
USA

British Library Cataloguing-in-Publication data.

Sladen, Christopher
    Conscription of Fashion: Utility Cloth,
    Clothing and Footwear, 1941–52
    I. Title
    941.084

Library of Congress Cataloging-in-Publication Data

Sladen, Christopher
    The conscription of fashion: utility cloth, clothing and
    footwear, 1941–52 / Christopher Sladen.
        p.   cm.
    Includes bibliographical references and index.
    ISBN 1–85928–007–2
    1. Costume—Great Britain—History—20th century. 2, Fashion—
    —Great Britain—History—20th century. 3. World War. 1939–1945—
    GT738.S53 1995
    391'.00941'09044—dc20   94–21964
                                    CIP

ISBN 1 85928 007 2

Typeset in Berkeley Old Style by Bournemouth Colour Graphics and printed in Great Britain at the University Press, Cambridge.

Contents

List of Tables

Acknowledgements

A great many people have contributed to the production of this book; my apologies to those whom I have inadvertently missed out.

During my research I was helped, advised and encouraged by librarians, archivists, curators and other staff from the following institutions and companies: Bath Museums Service; Bodleian Library, Oxford; Board of Trade/DTI; British Footwear Manufacturers Federation; British Library (Newspaper Library); British Textile Technology Institute; De Montfort University; Imperial War Museum; London Borough of Ealing; Marks & Spencer plc; Modern Records Centre, University of Warwick; Northampton Central Museum; Public Record Office, Kew; The Textile Institute; Victoria and Albert Museum. A sign of the times was the letter from the Curator of Blaise Castle House Museum, Bristol, politely regretting that access to the museum's collection of Utility clothes was impossible because of 'staff restructuring'.

Particular thanks are due to the archivists at the Mass Observation Archive, University of Sussex. Extracts from the Archive appear throughout this book: copyright the Trustees of the Mass Observation Archive, reproduced by permission of Curtis Brown Group Ltd.

I benefited from the advice of a number of acknowledged experts: June Swann on footwear; Nancy Richards on fashion and fabrics; Ismar Glasman on the work of Marks & Spencer. Harriet Dover, of the Geffrye Museum in London, and Kathy Niblett, City Museum, Stoke-on-Trent, explained how Utility affected furniture and tableware, respectively. My fellow Ealing resident Ellen Bretton reminisced usefully about her days in the Board of Trade during the 1940s. Any deductions and conclusions I may have drawn from all this, and any errors of fact are, of course, entirely my responsibility.

Permission to reproduce illustrations was kindly given by the following organizations: Bath Museums Service (Plate No. 9); Hulton Deutsch Collection Ltd (Plate Nos 1, 2, 3, and 4); Imperial War Museum (Plate Nos 6 and 7); Northampton Museum (Plate No. 5).

Finally, I should thank the editorial and other staff of Scolar Press for their unwavering tolerance and courtesy, and my family for their continuing interest during the years which this work has occupied me.

INTRODUCTION

Utility in Context

'In 1940 and the years which followed, the people of
Britain were protagonists in their own history in a fashion
never known before.'

Calder, *The People's War*

'The wartime picture is one of uniformity and drabness, the
atmosphere is austerity and the prevailing attitude is "Make
Do and Mend".'

Dorner, *Fashion in the Forties and Fifties*

This book is about one corner of life – Utility cloth, clothing, boots and
shoes – on the home front during the Second World War and the years
immediately after it. It looks at why and how Utility schemes were set up
and run by the Board of Trade, how they were received by manufacturers
and retailers, and what customers thought of Utility products. Reading
and writing about even this limited topic one constantly comes up
against major themes – strands common to all accounts of Second World
War civilian life – which spill over into the years after the war. Those
themes give the period its characteristic flavour, explaining, perhaps,
why it retains its fascination even 50 years later, and distinguish the
history of the Second War from that of the First.

The first and fundamental point is that, although the earlier war
was far more devastating in respect of casualties among the armed
forces, the reverse is true of civilians, as Table 1 shows:

Table 1   United Kingdom wartime fatalities

	1914–1918	*1939–1945*
Armed forces	744,000	264,000
Civilians	1,500	62,000

(Source: Taylor, 1965)

The 1939–1945 war was the first in which, from the outset, it was
clear that the civilian population was going to be directly involved.

1

The official history puts it as follows:

'The second world war ... was much less romantic than the first. It was a longer war, encompassing far more people; it was more sternly and austerely conducted and, except for some of the selfish ones, it was a more uncomfortable, physically upsetting war ... it imposed on a much larger part of the population the need to make a greater degree of adjustment in their personal lives.'[1]

This summary colours the way in which we look at individual restrictions, such as rationing, and how people reacted to them. It helps explain why Government took control on the home front more quickly and more energetically in the Second War than in the First, even though the natural preferences of many politicians may have changed comparatively little. In 1939 the Chamberlain Government began the war hoping that it would be short and could be fought and won with the minimum of social and economic dislocation. Chamberlain himself was by political conviction against restrictions on individuals or on firms. Despite this, his administration acted far more quickly than had its predecessor in 1914 in a number of ways: the almost immediate introduction of conscription is perhaps the outstanding example.

As hopes of a short war faded, the general realization of common peril and a common commitment to the war effort also implied a common willingness to accept the mass of controls and restrictions on corporate and private life. 'This was a people's war' is how it is summed up in A. J. P. Taylor's standard history of the 20th century.[2] Because Ministers and senior civil servants had lived through the earlier war, the need for government action of all kinds was better understood. Before 1914 Britain had not been directly involved in a European war for 60 years (even then it had been far away, in the Crimea). By contrast, no more than 20 years – the 'Long Weekend' of Graves and Hodge – passed between the end of the First and the opening of the Second World War.

During the 'phoney war' of 1939–1940 Ministers' hearts may not have been in civilian regimentation and government may not have been best organized to carry it out. Nevertheless, controls such as food rationing and price restriction were implemented almost immediately, by comparison with the First War, when they did not come into force until 1917; admittedly, a Ministry of Food had been set up before that, and Lord Devonport appointed as Food Controller, but he was said to have had 'no stomach for compulsory rationing', concentrating at first on prohibiting the display of luxury goods, including game.

Few people now remember Lord Devonport. By contrast his ebullient counterpart Fred Marquis, first Lord Woolton, has a secure place in the folklore of the Second World War. Woolton's own view was that 'Rationing and restrictions were introduced in the first world war to meet emergencies', whereas in the Second '... the planners had built up the conditions for a new Ministry [of Food] to operate at once'.[3] In 1914 the Asquith administration was strongly resistant to ideas of state intervention; Ministers '... had spent the greater part of their political careers in exploding the fallacies of Protectionism on the one hand and Socialism on the other'.[4] Small wonder, therefore, that the need for Government to encroach on the decisions of private firms took three years to sink home. But during the 1930s Government involvement, for example in regional policy and the running of utilities, had become recognized as at least a political possibility, even if a distasteful one to many Conservatives. The essentially defensive protectionism of that decade also provided a background to the concentration of industry in the Second World War, described in Chapter 1 of this book.

In 1939 the Government was able to draw not only on the experience of the First World War, but also of the long run-up to the Second, when events in central Europe and in Spain gave people a clear idea of what a new European war might involve. Britons, speculating about the consequences of defeat and occupation by German forces, were able to read accounts of life under such a regime (perhaps even meet refugees in person) during the latter half of the 1930s. The impact of air power, which people could visualize, for example from newsreels and newspaper accounts of the Spanish Civil War, meant that from the moment war was declared the civilian population thought of itself as in the front line.

The threat of this had been the subject of constant political and media discussion in the 1930s; by the middle of 1939 some 40 books about civil defence had been published in Britain. The fact that the need for these precuations was foreseen does not, of course, mean that central or local government, even when it acted quickly, necessarily acted efficiently or effectively. Doreen Idle's rapidly produced but compelling report, for the Fabian Society, on one borough of London[5] contains ample evidence of poor planning and political shenanigans in relation to shelter-building, advice and help centres, as well as other ARP matters.

With hindsight, we may think that the popular appeal of 'fair shares' and an acceptance of the need for sacrifices must have been powerful allies for the Government; '... the British people became a united nation in the face of perils which all shared', says Taylor.[6] A later historian, Peter Hennessy, concludes that the Government 'swiftly realised' that 'conspicuous fairness ... was indispensable to general public acceptance of institutionalised privation'.[7] 'Swiftly realised' does a kindness to those Ministers, like Churchill, who resolutely opposed rationing, but it is at least a plausible theory that solidarity on the home front helped cushion the restrictions, such as rationing and Utility, and that there was a contrast with civilian morale in the First World War; memories of shortages during that war became associated in the public's mind with unfair distribution and with profiteering.

Those who did not remember the First World War might draw comparisons between life in the 1930s, when high unemployment and poverty co-existed with affluence, and the shared hardship of the Second World War. Many people felt that a Britain in which, for example, no one except those who needed it most could buy new (Utility) furniture, though choice might be limited and design unexciting, was preferable to the pre-war contrast between the unemployed of Jarrow and the smart set of Mayfair. The poet Philip Larkin, when writing about 1940, shows no resentment in remembering limitations on Oxford undergraduate life: 'You see, nobody had anything in those days, in the war. There was one kind of jacket, one kind of trousers; no cars, one bottle of wine a term'.[8]

One other contrast between the First and Second World Wars, directly relevant to the content of this book, is the greater use made in 1939–1945 of sociological and market research techniques. British and other governments had used mass media during the First World War, to influence public opinion and to raise money to pay for the war. In 1939 the new and powerful medium of radio was available. But between the wars the development of market research by commercial firms represented an innovation in mass communication. The first Gallup poll took place in 1938. The setting up of Mass Observation added a new kind of semi-official, quasi-scientific body enquiring into, commenting on and analysing civilian morale; Mass Observation's founders stated early in the war their intention of keeping a full, accurate and objective record. A letter to the *Manchester Guardian* in October 1940 pointed out that 'It was not until well into the last war that the need for a permanent record of the military aspect was realised ... and a similar record of the home front was never even attempted'.[9]

Some historians see the growth of this kind of sociological activity as the key feature of the pre-war period: 'The singular thing about the Second World War was that the subject of morale among the civilian population ... was being considered long before ... war was certain'.[10] During the war Ministries built on this growth both to test reaction to new measures and to plan propaganda which might counteract rumour and uncertainty. Not all politicians believed in these new-fangled toys; Churchill was the arch-sceptic, at best uninterested in, often positively antagonistic to, the mass media and the idea of public opinion surveys. After 40 years at Westminster, the House of Commons was both the only sounding board and the only platform which he trusted.

Nevertheless, the scale of the home front intelligence effort was formidable; 'The compilers of [Ministry of Information] Home Intelligence Reports had a nationwide remit ... to present week in and week out a positive view of British morale'.[11] Among the sources which could be tapped were Government regional information officers, MPs' correspondence and news from the Whips' office, reports from Postal Censorship and from police duty rooms. BBC listener research, Citizens Advice Bureaux, the WVS and Mass Observation were non-official sources. Home Intelligence Reports, together with the more idiosyncratic ones from Mass Observation, contribute substantially to later chapters of this book. Thanks to all this activity, we do not today lack accounts covering every aspect of life on the home front in the Second World War – the first conflict in which what happened to civilians at home has been of as much interest to historians and the lay reader as the deeds of fighting men and their machines.

These general points, highlighting some of the ways in which civilian life in the Second World War was unique, provide our context. Within that we can look at the package of administrative measures affecting textiles, clothing and footwear, notably the Utility schemes. The Government wanted the package to achieve a number of objectives: to make best use of scarce raw materials; to free labour for the armed forces and for munitions work; to ensure a standard of living acceptable to the bulk of the civilian population, bolstering morale and preventing civil unrest. As we shall see, the Utility cloth and clothing scheme, introduced in 1941–1942, and the footwear scheme which followed soon after, were effectively add-ons to rationing and other controls in terms of raw material and production. They were innovative and had no real precedent in the First World War.

Eventually there were Utility schemes for cloth, clothing (including hosiery, gloves, braces and furs), footwear, household textiles, bedding and furniture. Imported timber, like wool and cotton, rapidly became scarce; the Government also wanted to release skilled labour from furniture factories. Furniture production was, indeed, more completely controlled than clothing or footwear. From 1943 to 1946 all furniture for civilian use was made to Utility designs produced by the Directorate of Furniture Production at the Board of Trade; the specifications fixed minimum standards of production and detailed design of the furniture. Demand was also strictly controlled.

As with cloth and clothing, advisory panels helped civil servants set up the Utility furniture scheme; the brief given to the furniture panel, including the eminent designer Gordon Russell, was simply to produce 'soundly made furniture, of the best available materials, and of pleasant design'. Although Utility furniture and clothing schemes had a great many similarities, there was an obvious difference in their impact. Everyone had to buy clothes, boots and shoes at some time during the war; the kind of survey we shall look at in later Chapters shows that an overwhelming majority included some Utility products among their purchases. By contrast only a minority of the population – principally those bombed out of their homes ('bombees' in ARP jargon) or newly-weds – were permitted to buy Utility furniture.

There were also a couple of minor and less obvious sectors – pencils and cigarette lighters – covered by Utility schemes. Again the motive was to reduce consumption of timber; since coal fires, gas cookers and cigarette smoking were the norm, matches were essential – lighters a substitute. Furniture, like cloth, clothing and footwear, had to carry the 'CC 41' Utility mark, whose origins are described in Chapter 2; pencils and lighters were simply too small to be marked in the same way but were nevertheless true Utility products.

There were other sectors where Government laid down rules (similar to the austerity restrictions on clothes, described in Chapter 1) for design and use of materials. The general public often referred to these products as 'Utility', but official records show that they were never classified as Utility, did not carry the Utility mark and were not automatically exempt from purchase tax – a major point which we will discuss in Chapter 5. Examples of these 'quasi Utility' products included tableware, glassware and holloware, standards for the last named of which were published by the Board of Trade in September 1941.

The story of Utility furniture is well told in Harriet Dover's book *Home Front Furniture* (Scolar Press, 1991) which examines the place of Utility in the broad sweep of design and popular taste. Kate Niblett's work on the history of the period, *Dynamic Design: the British Pottery Industry 1940–1990* (Stoke-on-Trent City Museum, 1990), documents the plain white 'Utility' china about which *Good Housekeeping* enthused at the time (August 1944): '... most is of beautiful design and some may well become period pieces'.

A Utility scheme, as Chapter 1 will illustrate, was only one of the weapons used by Government in the fight to make best use of raw materials and labour, prevent waste and keep the civil population content. In clothing there were also restrictions, laid down by the Board of Trade, on the *style* of men's and women's clothes. These restrictions, for example banning the use of turn-ups on men's trousers, applied both to Utility and non-Utility clothes, and were generally referred to as 'austerity' rules. In that sense the word 'austerity' had a precise interpretation; indeed, in this book 'austerity' and 'Utility' are generally used in this precise way. But both words could also be used more loosely and, not surprisingly, got confused in conversation and in memoirs of the period. In popular usage 'austerity' might imply a whole range of factors which depressed civilian life-style during and after the war: shortages, the black-out, rationing, restrictions on style, lack of colour, substitute materials and poor service (complaints about delays at laundries and dry cleaners are scattered through contemporary accounts).

Some of the 'austerities' were, of course, a good deal harder to bear than sluggish laundry service. Particularly when, in Chapter 5, we look at the situation immediately after the war, it is important to keep a sense of perspective; cuts in food rations and the lack of a roof over one's head were substantially more important than the inability to buy the style of clothes and shoes that one preferred. It was the cumulative effect of these restrictions, especially from 1945 onwards when people felt strongly that things should have been getting better, which added weight to criticism on individual measures.

In this book we look first at the factors which pushed the Government, against its natural inclinations, into regulating the cloth and clothing market, producing a package of measures (including rationing), many of which preceded the Utility scheme proper. Starting with experience in the First World War, it is possible to disentangle the origins of the Utility scheme itself; discussions among officials and Ministers which preceded its announcement in the summer of 1941 enable us to deduce what they hoped that this novel scheme would achieve.

Despite severe shortages of newsprint and manpower, Britain's newspapers and magazines, including fashion journals, continued to appear throughout the war. From them, and from the many subsequent histories of British fashion, we can build up a picture of how Utility clothes, made from Utility cloth, have been described by fashion writers and journalists. The surveys of Mass Observation and others give us an idea as to how Utility clothes were seen by the customers – and by the manufacturers and retailers on whom the Government depended to make the scheme work. It is important to remember that, although Ministers in the Board of Trade and elsewhere had what now seem wide-ranging powers to intervene in industry, factories and shops were not run by civil servants. Without the co-operation, sometimes grudging, sometimes willing, of entrepreneurs, retailers and trade associations, the Utility scheme and the Board of Trade's other industrial policies could not have worked; as we shall see, Utility cloth and clothing specifications were put together with the help of trade associations and others, including chain stores.

INTRODUCTION

As we shall also see, shortage of raw materials was a main driving force in bringing about the Utility clothing scheme; this was even more true in the case of boots and shoes, where imports of hides and rubber virtually ceased. As with clothes, producing the necessary specifications for Utility footwear depended on the co-operation of the trade. Boots and shoes, especially children's shoes, were, however, a source of much more public concern and controversy than was clothing in general. Production and retailing issues also differed. As with clothes, the sources from which we can deduce the impact and effectiveness of the Utility footwear scheme include social surveys, the popular press and the records of trade associations.

Although Utility, like rationing, was set up in response to the circumstances and needs of total war, it remained at least partially in place for more than six years after the war ended (rationing of food survived even longer). After 1945, however, the attitudes of customers, industry and of Government all changed. 'Austerity', in both its looser and more specific senses, had to be seen to be relaxed, even though Britain's economic problems, especially the dollar shortage, remained severe. Post-war, the history of the Utility scheme becomes much more embroiled with general economic and political themes. On the one hand we need to look more often at Parliamentary sources; on the other to take into account international fashion trends, notably the impact of the 'New Look' in 1947.

From all of these sources, and taking account of a couple of contemporary studies, it is possible to reach some conclusions, to summarize the contribution which Utility and the other parts of the package may have made to the Government's home front policy during the Second World War and afterwards. On rather less certain ground, perhaps, this book finishes by looking at the relationship between the style of Utility clothes, more especially women's outerwear, and the broad sweep of fashion and clothing manufacture in Britain.

NOTES

1   Titmuss, 1950, p348.
2   Taylor, 1965, p600.

3   Woolton, 1959, p179; the 'conditions' included identifying and recruiting Area Meat and Livestock Commissioners. Fred Marquis, as Chairman of Lewis's stores, was offered one of those necesary but low-profile jobs but declined, rightly expecting that his political connections would eventually produce a better offer.

4   E. M. Lloyd (1924), quoted in Stevenson, 1984, p69.

5   Doreen Idle's *War Over West Ham* (Faber 1944) contrasts the preparedness and efficiency of the Borough of West Ham with those of its neighbouring local authorities and is a neglected classic of the period.

6   Taylor, 1975, p76.

7   Hennessy, 1992, p50.

8   Larkin, interview with *The Observer*, reprinted in *Required Writing*, 1985.

9   Harrison and Madge, 1940, p15. Mass Observation (MO) had been formed in 1937 by Tom Harrison, Charles Madge and Humphrey Jennings to study the everyday lives of ordinary people in Britain. Early work was based partly in Bolton ('Worktown'), partly in London. MO used teams of paid investigators to record people's conversations and behaviour in public places; a panel of volunteer observers throughout Britain also kept diaries and replied to monthly questionnaires. Information from both sources formed the basis for around 3,000 MO reports. Many of them are on aspects of life on the home front and record reactions to restrictions such as rationing and Utility during the war. The Ministry of Information paid MO to monitor civilian morale in 1940–1941.

10   Titmuss, 1950, p338.

11   Calder, 1991, p100.

CHAPTER 1

Clothes, Coupons and Concentration: Civilian Clothing Policy in General

'Into this [pre-war] motley scene of trade, in which merchants struggled with each other to please consumers, rich and poor, young and old, chic and frumpish ... came the war, the greatest consumer of all, like a giant tapeworm, exacting, changeable, insatiate.'
Wadsworth, *Review of Economic Studies,* 1948

'When you are tired of your old clothes, remember that by making them do you are contributing some part of an aeroplane, a gun or a tank.'
Oliver Lyttleton, President of the Board of Trade, introducing clothes rationing, 1 June 1942

The Utility cloth, clothing and footwear schemes represented major strands in the Government's package of measures aimed at providing durable civilian clothing and shoes at an affordable price; they were, however, inextricably linked to other parts of that package. Before looking at Utility in detail it is useful to set the scene, first by taking a quick look at the clothing and fashion industries in general, then at other aspects of the Government's civilian clothing policy.

The 1930s had in fact been a period of great activity and some success, at least for parts of those industries. Apart from the ever-present influence of Paris (Chanel and Edward Molyneux were in full flow), couture fashion was on the move in London; those designers whom we will see drafted in to work on Utility – Hartnell, Morton, Amies – and who are still household names today, derived their reputations from that period. The look of women's clothes had changed substantially at the end of the 1920s, skirt lengths plummeting almost as startingly as had share prices on Wall Street in 1929 ('Bomb drops – skirts reach ankles', was *Vogue's* headline). The boyish look of the 1920s disappeared; waists and feminine curves were back in place. Through the 1930s the fashion historian Elizabeth Ewing then detects relatively few major changes; the biggest innovation was perhaps the introduction of the backless evening dress which, combined with back

11

drapings on bodice and skirt, made it look as though the wearer were entering the room backwards.[1] Because more middle-class women worked, either in the home or outside, day-time clothes became more practical, evening wear by comparison more glamorous. White tie and tails for men and low-cut evening dress for women were familiar both in private houses, restaurants and at the theatre.

Squared padded shoulders, whose introduction in 1936 is usually credited to Schiaparelli, were popular; they remained characteristic of Utility and other wartime women's jackets and coats. The anonymous writer in the *DR* (Drapers' Record) *Centenary Supplement* (1987) sees them as the only 'hint of plenty' in the 1940's fashion scene, which was otherwise characterized by economy of fabric, shorter, straighter skirts, 'perhaps with a few skimpy pleats'. In the 1930s London enjoyed a period of dominance in respect of sportswear and beachwear, the market for which was boosted by the increase in foreign travel and the relative affluence of the middle class; *Vogue* advised its readers to take at least three bathing suits to the beach each day.[2] In men's fashions, the shape, materials and colours of lounge suits, sports jackets and flannels did not vary significantly through the 1930s. Single or double breasted, with shoulders more or less built up, lapels and trouser widths widening or narrowing; there was little excitement for male customers. It was not unreasonable that, as we shall see, politicians and civil servants should assume that most men would be relatively indifferent to rationing and Utility.

Although the appearance of clothes might have changed little, there were substantial changes in the way they were made, bought and sold. Import duties, imposed as part of the National Government's protectionist policy in the early 1930s, gave a fillip to British textiles as a whole. Within the industry, couture fashion was losing some of its status. Ready-to-wear clothing, mass produced by factory methods, had become a more significant part of the trade of stores, large and small, by the 1930s. After the great impetus to women's employment during the First World War, more and more women had jobs either in the new, clean, electric-power factories or in offices. Following the example set in the US, some manufacturers began to sell fashions under their own brand names. The future challenge to the dominance of the departmental stores was beginning, with the growth of specialist chain stores; numbers increased from 300 in the 1920s to over 1,300 by 1939. Marks and Spencer started to take fashion seriously, learning from American example, moving towards a concentration on women's and children's clothes and developing a close relationship with their suppliers in terms of design, quality and cost.

The outbreak of war in 1939 sent a shock-wave throughout the textile and fashion industries, as through other sectors. The First World War had brought about a rapid simplification of women's clothes, both because materials were scarce and because women took jobs and needed more freedom of movement. Slender figures became more admired and, says Madge Garland, 'Voluptuous curves disparaged [as] the comfortable elasticised pull on girdle and separate brassière made their appearance';[3] few middle class women were immediately attracted by trousers (as advocated by the Rational Dress movement). Factory girls did wear trousers – baggy ones under thick cotton overalls – plus mob caps. Tailor-made costumes developed a military look. The war gave an impetus to the long-term levelling process in women's fashions. Importantly, social and fashion historians agree that there was a steady decline in quality; avoiding this would be one of the Government's aims in 1941.

In 1939, as in 1914, politicians and journalists rushed to hoist the 'business as usual' flag – the 'carry on signal', a *Vogue* editorial called it – rationalizing the inevitably tighter and shorter style in women's wear in the phrase: 'Il faut SKIMP pour être chic'.[4] *Vogue* itself, like other periodicals, was forcibly slimmed in terms of both size and frequency. As 1940 began the tone remained determinedly jolly; intrepid journalists were in Paris for the collections of January 1940. Just over a year later and only two months before clothes were rationed, *Picture Post's* March 1941 cover showed a spring hat; there was also a feature on women's nightwear which managed to avoid mentioning air raids, shelter life and other deprivations, referring only to woolly bed-jackets as a blessing for women who liked to make their own clothes.

Struggling to summarize the view taken by fashion historians regarding the design of women's clothes in the Second World War, we might hit upon 'restraint and practicality': the silhouette a plain rectangle, box-shaped jackets, padded shoulders, narrow skirts and a generally severe outline.[5] For women in factories, slacks and jumpers were undoubtedly practical; 'restraint' was perhaps less apt when applied to the 1940's equivalent of the First World War mob cap – the turban or coloured scarf – Jacqmar, if you could get it. Jacqmar did its bit for propaganda with a 'Laurières de la Victoire' design selling at 55/10 (£2.80); in similar vein cotton dress material was printed with the national flags of Britain's allies or with slogans such as 'Dig for Victory'. While most people probably saw the flowering of brightly coloured headwear as no more than a marriage of practicality and optimism, others took a more jaundiced view, seeing it as evidence that the English, 'now that their living standard was reduced to that of the poor East European peasant, emulated them by tying handkerchiefs round their heads'.[6] The heroine of Elizabeth Bowen's novel, *The Heat of the Day* (Faber 1949), attending an open air concert in 1942, was described as having taken 'a flying try at the Soviet comrade type' in her choice of dress.

Any influence from eastern Europe, conscious or unconscious, was more than balanced by the continuous barrage of innovations from across the Atlantic, of which socks and shorts for women were examples. The United States government, too, imposed restrictions on clothing production: prices were controlled from 1943; manufacturers had to produce a proportion of cheaper lines; the War Production Board aimed for a 15 per cent reduction in use of materials; there were style restrictions; the L85 regulations banned the use of double yokes, sashes, patch pockets and other embellishments. All this, however, left the American industry with plenty of scope both for experiment and expansion; indeed, it is claimed that the loss of contact with Paris, on which the US fashion industry had depended, gave a boost to the confidence of American designers and manufacturers, paving the way for expansion in the later 1940s.

Alongside coverage of such new clothes as came onto the market, the London media provided regular hints on substitute materials. Straightforward advice on how to adapt good quality clothes was supplemented by anecdotes – recycled almost as often as the clothes themselves – about ingenious substitutes for dress materials, including furnishing fabrics, blackout material, blankets (women who had coats adapted from RAF blankets felt themselves a cut above those with Army blanket material). Among the less likely material said to have been used was old Ordnance Survey map linen; a *Sunday Chronicle* 'girl reporter' claimed to have made a whole suit out of heavy grey whipcord salvaged from old car seat covers. Unsurprisingly, by 1943 a Mass Observation survey found that women were spending more time on repairs, alterations, generally making-do, and visiting more jumble sales and WVS 'clothing exchanges' than pre-war; they also expected, once the war was over, to dress more simply and buy for quality, rather than for show.

This is the background against which the Government's textile and clothing policy was set. Before examining, in the next chapter, the part played by Utility, we can summarize other aspects of that policy, with special emphasis on those restrictions of which the consumer was most directly aware. Apart from Utility, these included: the *allocation* of raw materials, *price control*, *concentration* of firms (in textile and other sectors), *rationing* and *restrictions on style*. Most of these other measures preceded Utility; the austerity restrictions on style were not introduced until later (May 1942) but it is convenient to deal with them too as part of the 'pre-Utility' package. A contemporary article tabulated the initial moves in all this. The essay by P. Ady, '*Utility Goods*' in *Studies in War Economics* (1942), set out three stages of civilian clothing control; his overview is reproduced below as Table 1.1.

The Government needed to do several things at the same time: to keep prices down; to make sure the civilian population was reasonably clad; to prevent unrest on the home front and keep up morale; as well as to avoid waste of scarce resources – manpower and raw materials. Fear that the cost of living would shoot out of control was a powerful spur to action early in the war. Shortages of materials and labour, coupled with rising wages as the unemployed took up jobs created by the war effort and as overtime increased, all meant that clothing and other prices rose rapidly between 1939 and 1941. By March 1941 the general cost of living index was up by 29 per cent compared with the immediate pre-war level, but the clothing component of the index showed a 69 per cent increase and was still rising. Cloth warehouses had been destroyed in the blitz and stocks were low. In his 1941 Budget speech the Chancellor of the Exchequer (Kingsley Wood) said that the Government aimed: 'To prevent any further rise in the cost of living index number, apart from minor seasonal changes, above the range of 125–130 in terms of the pre-war level'.[7]

The Government was worried by memories of the First World War when the cost of living for unskilled workers rose by 80 per cent between 1914 and 1918. Combined with other grievances – conscription, rent increases, narrowing pay differentials, and 'dilution' (including the introduction of female labour) - this caused discontent to boil over in 1917. Working-class families, most with members in the armed forces, drew bitter comparisons between the privations of the many and the comparative affluence of the few at home. Economic discontent slipped into political unrest: popular agitators were excited by events in Russia, the Triple Alliance of railwaymen, miners and transport workers, was revived and Clydeside took on its 'Red' hue. A series of Commissions of Enquiry during the First World War had confirmed that high prices were a significant cause of the unrest. Government action, apart from being late, was generally indirect and

15

Table 1.1 The development of civilian clothing control

	Stages.	a: Quantitative Control a	b: Quality Control b	c: Price Control c
		Table 1, To October 31st, 1941.		
1	Raw Materials to *Manufacturer*	Allocation of raw materials ration for Home Civilian Trade by *Controls* (less rigid for cotton than for wool)		Fixing of Home Trade Issue Prices of raw wool, cotton, etc., by appropriate Control.
2	Cloth from Manufacturer to *Clothier* or *Wholesaler*			*All types of cloth.* Method of calculation of cost of production and profit margins fixed under agreement between *Textile Manufacturers Delegations & Central Price Regulation Committee.*
3	Cloth or clothing from Manufacturer, Wholesaler or Clothier to *Retailer*	Quantities of sales restricted on a percentage basis under Limitation of Supplies Orders		*All types of cloth.* Check – "Prices of Goods' Act, 1939.
4	Cloth or clothing from Retailer to *Consumer*	Against coupons under Consumer Rationing Orders, June 1941		*All types of clothing.* Check – 'Prices of Goods' Act, 1939.
		Table II. November 1st to June 1st, 1942		
1	Raw Materials to *Manufacturer*	As Table 1 1a Special Quota for Utility Cloth separated from General Home Civilian Quota and graded up in a priority scheme		As Table 1 1c.
2	Cloth from Manufacturer to *Clothier* or *Wholesaler*		Provisional emergency standards of minimum quality for *Utility Cloth* but in many cases defined only by price limit	*All types as Table 1 2c. Utility.* Over-riding maximum prices for Utility Cloth under Utility Cloth (Max. Prices) Order

3	Cloth or clothing from Manufacturer, Wholesaler or Clothier to *Retailer*	As Table 1 3a	Provisional emergency standards for Utility Cloth and directions for making-up Clothing	*All types* as Table I 3c *Utility.* Manufacturers', makers-up and Wholesalers' profit margins fixed, with over-riding maximum prices at each stage under Utility Apparel (Max. Prices) Orders
4	Cloth or clothing from retailer to *Consumer*	As Table 1 4a		*All Types* as Table I 4c *Utility.* Retailers' profit margins fixed, with over-riding maximum price

Table III. Since June 1st, 1942.

1	Raw Materials to *Manufacturer*	Special Quota for Utility Cloth as Table II 1a. Released by appropriate Control to manufacturer against presentation of sub-certificates up to total ration of Home Civilian Trade		As Table I 1c
2	Cloth from Manufacturer to *Clothier or Wholesaler*	Cloth supplied by manufacturer directly, or indirectly, through merchant, against clothing sub-certificate. These last are issued by clothier against 'key' certificate of estimated Utility cloth requirements. 'Key' certificates issued by Control under authorization of Board of Trade.	Govt. guaranteed quality standards issued by B.S.I. C.C. 41, in many cases still defined only by price and type	From August 3rd *Non-utility,* Manufacturers' and makers-up prices fixed at level of June 30th, 1942 *Utility,* as Table II 2c
3	Cloth or clothing from Manufacturer, Clothier or Wholesaler to *Retailer*	Against coupons	Govt. guaranteed quality stds. C.C.41 *All types:* Rules simplifying styles. Directions for making-up Utility	From August 3rd *Non-utility.* Wholesalers' profit margins fixed under General Approval & Cloth (Max. Prices & Charges) Order. *Utility.* As Table II 3c Purchase Tax remitted
4	Cloth or clothing from retailer to *Consumer*	Against coupons as Table I 4a		From August 3rd *Non-Utility.* Retailers' profit margins fixed *Utility.* As Table II 4c

Reproduced from 'Utility Goods' by P. Ady, in *Studies in War Economics*, Blackwell, 1942, by permission of the publishers.

ineffective. Boards of control were set up for the wool and cotton industries, to oversee allocation of raw materials; cotton production was cut to 60 per cent of its pre-1914 level, but without positive efforts to improve efficiency and without effective rationing.

The lesson of 1917 therefore seemed to be that keeping prices under control, allied to 'fair shares' and equality of misery, might pay dividends in terms of morale and economic efficiency. In due course, a 1942 Ministry of Information survey, intended to test reaction to rationing, did seem to show that the great majority of civilians were prepared to face sacrifices of all kinds provided they thought that the Government was making real efforts, and that the burden of restrictions and shortages was seen to be fairly borne. The first step was to control raw materials. By May 1940, despite Chamberlain's reluctance to intervene in the market, the Government had become the sole importer of nearly 90 per cent of all raw materials, including wool. Allocating those imports to individual firms was the job of the 'Controls' operated by the Ministries of Supply and Food. The Wool Control, which operated from 1940 to 1949, started by buying up all the wool available on the market in Australia, New Zealand and South Africa and shipping it back to Britain, providing an invaluable buffer stock for the middle of the war, when virtually no new supplies could get through. The full story of the 'Controls' is told in the volume of the official history *Control of Raw Materials* by Hurstfield (HMSO, 1953).

The use which manufacturers could make of their allocations was first, and ineffectually, subject to a broad control on output, to try and limit the volume of garments coming onto the market. An Order (*Limitation of Supplies (Miscellaneous) Order*, 6 June 1940, often abbreviated to LIMOSO) was made under which manufacturers and wholesalers applied to the Board of Trade for registration; once registered they were assigned quotas which fixed the total value of clothing which they could supply, based on past sales in a given six-month period. At that stage the Government's preference was still to avoid rationing. Price control had already been introduced early in the war by the *Prices of Goods Act* 1939, but this had little effect on the clothing sector where it was too difficult to specify the items to which the control applied. Manufacturers quickly switched to production of lines plainly *not* subject to price control. Without direct control over production and without specific definitions of the products, price control would always be ineffective. In the end the general run-down in stocks, allied to the deliberate policy of limiting supplies, naturally resulted in prices continuing to climb.

Next, in March 1941 the President of the Board of Trade (Oliver Lyttleton) published a White Paper[8] announcing that production of 'less essential' goods would be subject to 'concentration'. In a number of sectors (eventually 50, including some, such as soft drinks and building materials, administered by other Ministries) only a reduced number of 'nucleus' factories would be allowed to continue full-time working; production from others would be transferred to the 'nucleus' plants, although their machinery would be kept intact, and those firms continuing to produce had to make financial arrangements to compensate them. 'Nucleus' factories were offered some safeguards against losing labour to munitions work or having plant requisitioned; they could also expect a more secure supply of raw materials – provided they produced what the Board of Trade wanted them to.

Although civil servants decided on the degree of concentration in each sector, nearly all the schemes were voluntary and the choice of which factories should survive and which should be moth-balled was taken on the advice of industry bodies. The usual procedure was for a group of firms to select one of its number to produce on behalf of the rest, although occasionally the group would pool resources and create a new firm to produce on behalf of the group as a whole; the lace industry was one example. Cotton-spinning firms were selected by the Cotton Control. Officials at first believed that it would be too difficult to concentrate garment-makers because they were too widespread, with too many small firms. Pressure from the Ministry of Supply's Factory and Storage Control, however, led to arrangements being made, at first town by town, later by region and then nationally, by which the Wholesale Fashion Trades Association became responsible for 'introducing' firms to one another. Concentration impacted sharply on the textile and footwear industries: by 1944 it was estimated that 65 per cent of the labour released, and 60 per cent of the factory space saved, had come from four sectors: wool, cotton, clothing, boots and shoes. Concentration should logically have complemented the Utility scheme where, as we shall see, a limited number of firms were *designated* by the Board of Trade but, in fact, practice fell short of this ideal.

The public at large may have known little about concentration. Rationing, however, was both visible and controversial. It was an obvious 'fair shares' device, one very often referred to in histories and memoirs. Food rationing had been introduced in January 1940 (to start with clothes rationing made use of spare food coupons). The Conservative press, especially the *Daily Express*, opposed rationing and, perhaps influenced by Beaverbrook, Churchill too resisted it, whether for food or clothes. When clothes rationing and 'standard' dress (see Chapter 2) were under discussion, Churchill accused Lyttleton of wanting to 'strip the poor people to the buff'. Lyttleton later claimed that clothes rationing had only slipped past Churchill when the latter was absorbed in the hunt for the *Bismarck*.[9] In any event, a basic clothes ration of 66 coupons per adult was announced on 1 June 1941; there were some later variations on this and on the coupon value of individual garments. Apart from appealing to people's sense of fairness, rationing was economically efficient, since it ensured that supplies followed the shifting population around the country; the more coupons a shopkeeper received, the larger his subsequent order for new goods.

Reaction ranged from outrage through indifference to enthusiasm. Many workers claimed that the ration would not cover work needs: the National Union of Agricultural Workers said farm workers would need, as a minimum, 133 coupons a year; Ministry of Labour statisticians, looking at what farm workers had actually bought pre-war, thought that 60 was nearer the mark.[10] Without the benefit of statistics the couturier Digby Morton, interviewed by Mass Observation, concluded that: '... in the country people don't need their coupons so much ... village people on estates and so on'. More generally, Mass Observation found that after a couple of months 75 per cent of men and 43 per cent of women were in favour of clothes rationing; 'good work', 'equality of sacrifice', 'fairness' and even 'congratulate the Board of Trade' were among positive comments from MO diarists. There was, however, some evidence of poor public relations by the Board of Trade and one interviewee perceptively complained that rationing was no good without better price control, even if that meant the introduction of 'standardised stuff'.[11]

The difference in attitude between the sexes (more accurately, the male view of that difference) was epitomized by Lyttleton when he introduced rationing: 'I know all the women will look smart', he said, 'but we men may look shabby. If we do, we must not be ashamed. In war the term "battle stained" is an honourable one.' Two of Mass Observation's anonymous male interviewees, one a local government official and the other a railway porter, confided that 'I like comfort, but my wife likes me to be smart' and 'I'd go around in anything, I wouldn't care what people thought, but my wife likes to keep me up to the mark'.[12] Representing a different segment of the market, a fourth leader in *The Times* (3 September 1941) thought that 'Better off people' were 'largely giving up evening and special clothes', and men were 'using up sports clothes for spare wear, without replacing them'. Lyttleton's fellow Tory MP Sir Henry ('Chips') Channon, recorded in his diary:

> 'The big news this morning is clothes rationing. Oliver Lyttleton is only going to allow us 66 coupons per annum. A suit takes 26. Luckily I have 40 or more [i.e. suits]. Socks will be the shortage. Apart from those, if I am not bombed, I have enough clothes to last me for years.'[13]

The indefatigable Mollie Panter-Downes, recording the London wartime scene for the *New Yorker*, shrewdly noted that:

> '... this new step will mean writing off hundreds of small businesses. ... If you ... walk down any London shopping street you are likely to see shutters over the windows of dozens of modest businesses, which struggled through the blitz but couldn't survive rationing.'[14]

The Board of Trade's public relations campaign, on whose effectiveness the MO survey cast doubts, included an imaginary civil servant, 'Mr Nicholas Davenport', who was heard on the BBC admonishing a young lady colleague to 'Cut your clothes according to your coupons' and 'Never coupon today what you can put off until tomorrow'. An annual 'Clothing Quiz' published by HMSO at 2d (1p), while primarily a guide to the allocation and use of clothes coupons, promised 'Useful hints, tested and approved by the Make Do and Mend Advisory Panel on preservation of clothes and household linen'. There were similar private sector publications.[15] The 'Make Do and Mend' slogan was taken up widely in the press, both in editorial columns and advertisements. An advertisement for Lux soap flakes insisted that 'The best parts of worn out net curtains make lovely brassières – ones that have a pre-war French accent!' *Vogue* (July 1941) ran a feature on how to 'Refresh a coupon-based wardrobe' with hats and other accessories. Even with the best efforts of 'Nicholas Davenport' and his colleagues, however, the addition of rationing to the previous controls was not enough to achieve what the Government wanted – to keep down the cost of living. As the coupon value was fixed according to the amount of cloth in the garment, both manufacturers and consumers were encouraged to spend more by concentrating on the more durable – and more expensive – types of clothing.

The final part of civilian clothing control, other than Utility, was the series of restrictions on style, whose aim was to simplify designs and so save material – and, of course, contribute to cost-saving. Although it was not always appreciated at the time, all of these 'austerity' regulations applied equally to Utility and non-Utility garments. A series of Orders (*Civilian Clothing (Restrictions) Orders*) covered most items of clothing, starting in May 1942 when restrictions were placed on trimmings, pockets and trouser turn-ups on men's and boys' wear. Hugh Dalton foreshadowed this last and much debated feature when answering a Parliamentary question on 10 March; having agreed that prohibition of turn-ups should be considered, he assured his questioner that he personally never asked for turn-ups when ordering trousers.[16] Dalton's boast that doing without turn-ups was both patriotic and stylish got unexpected support from editorials in the *Daily Mail* which claimed that pre-war 'Plain bottoms [without turn-ups] were the prerogative of the fellow who spent a lot of time in front of the mirror' whereas in wartime, thanks to Dalton, such stylishness could be enjoyed by all. *The Times*, tracing the origins of the turn-up to the muddy roads of pre-macadam days, called the 20th-century survival 'a mere tailored pretence. Let it go, by all means.' And when, in 1944, these restrictions were largely abandoned (see Chapter 5), *The Times* suggested that although 'The question of turn-ups may have caused more bitter and derisive comment', in practical terms it was 'the deprivation of pockets that has been hardest to bear'.

Other restrictions on men's wear included a maximum length for shirts and, in hosiery, for socks. Shortage of hosiery was a real problem for many men, as 'Chips' Channon had predicted; in his autobiography, *I Play As I Please* (1954), Humphrey Lyttleton claimed that his uncle, a steel company executive, gave up wearing socks altogether, travelling into the City on the Underground each day with a large area of naked skin showing below the bottom of his pin-striped trousers. In women's outerwear the number of pleats, seams, buttons and buttonholes was limited, and maximum widths fixed for sleeves, belts, hems and collars. Decorative additions such as embroidery, fur or leather on outerwear and ornamental stitching on underwear, were prohibited; official historians have suggested that the saving of material was probably small, although the restrictions did help speed up production. Dalton's claim was more ambitious: 'The economy of material due to the prohibition of turn-ups runs into millions of square feet a year'.[17]

A third class of restrictions prohibited the use of specified raw materials.

The *Elastic (Control of Use) Order* (1943, No. 90), for example, prohibited the use of elastic in all garments except women's corsets and knickers; as rubber became more readily available this order, like others, was relaxed, but a Government leaflet in 1945 still needed to advise women that elastic was on war service and '... when your suspenders wear out, cut away the worn part and replace with an inch or two of strong tape or braid'.[18] To encourage long production runs of garments with a strong fashion element, a limit was put on the number of basic designs which could be made by any firm in any year. Manufacturers of women's dresses were restricted to 50 sets of basic style templates per year; girls' dresses were even more sharply confined to 15 styles. In the production of overalls the Board of Trade approached most closely to a real policy of standardization since none could be made unless they conformed to BoT specifications.

Lastly there were restrictions which, rather than negative prohibitions, were positive requirements, designed to set minimum standards in relation to the sizing and making up of garments – for example the standard of sewing to be used in the case of women's underwear and nightwear. This positive element of style restrictions and the direct involvement of Government in the design of clothing were two of the central features of the Utility scheme itself, to which we can now turn.

NOTES

1   Ewing, 1974, p111.
2   *Vogue*, 1991, p57; in the 1950s *Vogue's* advice would be different: stick to the same swimsuit all the time and ensure an even tan.
3   Garland, 1983, p229.
4   *Vogue*, 1991, p 69.
5   Cunnington, 1952, p150; Cunnington goes on to give a more detailed description: 'Tailor made jacket, 25" long, shoulders broad and padded, cuffless 2-piece sleeve, skirt 16/17" from the ground, slim but often slightly flared or pleated. Hipline kept flat, waistline smoothly fitted by darts and seams. Materials – tweeds, flannel, plain or pin-striped, gaberdines'. Cunnington says that femininity was sustained by afternoon and dinner dresses with hip drapery and skirts hanging in folds nearly to the ground.
6   Garland, 1983, p244.
7   HofC, Vol. 370, Cols 1320–1322.

8   *Concentration of Production*, Cmnd 6258, March 1941. A full
    description of the policy of concentration may be found in essays by
    G. C. Allen and G. N. Worswick in the NIESR/Cambridge University
    Press publication *Lessons of the British War Economy*, 1952. Allen,
    Professor of Political Science, University of Liverpool 1933–1947, had
    been a temporary Assistant Secretary in the Board of Trade
    1941–1944. A 1944 review of concentration is covered in PRO BT
    96/127 and BT 190/1.
9   Lyttleton (Chandos), 1962, p205.
10 PRO, BT 64/76.
11 M-OA, File reports 35A, 756, 830, June–Aug. 1941, and *Change No.
    1*, produced by MO for *Advertising Service Guild.*
12 M-OA, *Change No. 1*, p83.
13 Channon, 1967, p307.
14 Panter-Downes, 1971, p153.
15 For example, *New Clothes From Old*, Evans Brothers, 1944; Selfridges
    advertised its Coupon Advisory Bureau in women's magazines.
16 HofC, Vol. 376, Col. 906; Dalton made another virtue out of necessity
    in the case of hats: his *Diaries* (p484, 27 Aug. 1942) record his
    satisfaction that 'we shall soon have no more hats and everyone with
    natural hair should go about without one'. An anonymous but
    spirited BoT official minuted Dalton suggesting that by the same
    token those with beards should be encouraged to do without collar
    and tie. Lord Longford, reminiscing about Dalton in 1993,
    remembered best the latter's anti-hat campaign which was perhaps
    not unconnected with the antipathy between Dalton and the hat-
    loving Eden.
17 HofC, Vol. 387, Col. 1204; Dalton's *Diaries* (p528) record that George
    VI, at least, remained unimpressed by these claims; the monarch
    showed little interest in Utility, but was worried by the concentration
    policy, having heard rumours that the BoT planned to shift
    production of straw hats from Luton to the North East: Dalton sat for
    a Durham constituency. George VI also took the opportunity to
    complain about increases in the price of silver cigarette boxes and
    other items which he liked to buy and use as gifts.
18 That rubber was later freed for other garments is evidenced by the
    author's pair of Utility braces, complete with the CC 41 mark, still in
    excellent working order. The Utility braces scheme, although
    categorized by BoT as a minor one, remained in place until 1952.

CHAPTER 2

'Standard', 'Essential', 'Utility': Origins and Development of Utility Cloth and Clothing

'The Utility scheme ... has always been a matter of ... controversy and interest. Owing nothing to control devices in other countries ... it has never ... been copied.'
Wadsworth, *Review of Economic Studies*, 1948

'The word Utility has become a noble title.'
Hugh Dalton, President of the Board of Trade, 1942

By spring 1940 Ministers were talking, with some distaste, about a scheme for 'standard' clothing; the term dated from the First World War but as with rationing, it had surfaced only fleetingly and late in the war, reflecting the Government's reluctance to interfere with the market. Among the few specific measures then taken was an order, made in the winter of 1918, fixing a limit of 4.5 yards of woollen cloth for women's dresses; *Vogue* recommended its readers to slim and to wear silk instead. Earlier that year a 'National Standard Dress' for civilians was proposed and at least one 'utility (*sic*) garment' was said to have been produced, with metal buckles instead of hooks and eyes, designed to serve all purposes – 'outdoor gown, house gown, rest gown, tea gown, dinner gown, evening dress and night gown'.[1]

The clothing trade was aware that a more general 'Standard Goods Scheme' was under discussion within Government, but by November 1918 the only tangible output was a small quantity of 'standard' blankets, winter hosiery and underwear in the shops. The *Drapers' Record* said the latter were of 'excellent quality' and added that there was 'loose talk of standard materials for women's skirts and dresses'; another proposal was that surplus 'shell cloth' (woollen serge) would be bought by the Government and given to makers-up for women's costumes for sale at fixed prices. Finally, a limited number of men's suits were produced from 'standard' cloth, virtually all of which went to demobilized servicemen. As the war was then over, it was not surprising that neither trade nor consumer could be interested in any of these ideas.

The creation of women's services and the need to provide them with uniforms were more significant, from the point of view both of fashion and social history and of precedent for the Second World War. Women police, the Womens Auxiliary Army Corps (WAAC) and the Womens Land Army (WLA) were all in being by 1916. The WAAC alone attracted 50,000 volunteers in its first few months. Many of the poorer volunteers had to be turned down, mostly because they were not robust enough but in some cases because they did not have enough underwear to go with their uniforms. The WLA uniform of knickerbockers and leggings under an overall was adapted from traditional farm-workers' clothing.

At the start of the Second World War Ministers, notably Churchill, were as strongly opposed to 'standard' dress as to rationing (with some inconsistency, Churchill then became a keen advocate of the utilitarian 'siren suit', an all-in-one garment with zip front). There were a few voices in favour of the idea that civilians too should go into uniform; its supporters may have seen themselves as heirs of the 'rational dress' movement, promoted by Shaw and the Fabians – a good enough reason for Conservative Ministers to be suspicious. In any event, such a radical approach was quickly rejected on grounds of drabness and of morale. It would also have been unsound economically since the vast amount of wear left in existing clothing would have been largely wasted; moreover, if the uniform had been stout enough for civilians in heavy manufacturing jobs, it would have been far too hard-wearing for everyone else.

In view of the natural antipathy of politicians, it is therefore surprising that 'standard' clothing was on the agenda when the war was only six months old. As early as January 1940 rumours were circulating about the likelihood of 'pool' (that is, mass-made) clothing.[2]

On 7 March 1940 a meeting of the War Cabinet Ministerial Committee on Economic Policy (EP(M)), chaired by the Chancellor of the Exchequer, Sir John Simon, considered a paper[3] on the subject of standard cloth and clothing, prepared by an interdepartmental group of officials who acknowledged advice from Lord Woolton, 'specially qualified in this respect' (at that point he was in the Ministry of Supply advising on how to secure production of army uniforms and boots).

The paper dealt only with men's suits. It envisaged a scheme which would operate through production of a 'standard cloth', using wool bought by the Government, sold to makers-up on condition that they would make suits for a set profit margin and sell them on to retailers under a resale price agreement. The eventual price to the customer would be determined by cost of production (that is, 'cost plus'). It was left open whether the retail price might in time need to be held down by subsidy – as food prices already were.

Woolton's advice was that the scheme ought to cover women's and children's wear, as well as men's, and footwear as well as clothes. Any scheme would be valuable only if people believed that prices would be fixed. Initially, he thought, a 'standard' suit would be unlikely to cost less than those made by the big manufacturers, but the scheme would still be worthwhile because the cost of a 'Government suit' would prevent large makers-up from increasing their own prices and making 'unreasonable' profits. Woolton expected 'substantial profiteering' if the 'standard suits' scheme did not go ahead.

Woolton was not a member of the Ministerial Committee. Those who were showed no enthusiasm. 'Standard suits', it was pointed out, would still be in competition with manufacturers' other products, and if it was true that they could produce as cheaply as the Government, what was the point of the scheme? On the other hand, if the 'standard suit' was priced to undercut the regular lines, this would represent unfair competition. Further, keeping down the price of clothing would simply encourage extra consumption, 'inappropriate' in wartime. In any case, the paper did not indicate how important men's suits were to cost-of-living calculations; perhaps men would only buy new suits for Sunday best? Women's and children's clothes might be more important economically, but Ministers could not conceive that they too might be 'standardized'. All in all the Committee did not think the scheme would have much effect on the index.

Despite this lukewarm discussion, however, Ministers recommended that in principle a scheme should be got ready for the autumn of 1940, covering standard cloth for suits and, less certainly, standard boots and shoes. Ministers thought the work should be handled by the Raw Materials Department of the Ministry of Supply. In the end, however, the main job of devising the scheme went to the Industries and Manufactures (IM) Department of the Board of Trade.[4]

From the outset the Government was keen to play down the concept of standardization; as late as 16 July 1941 the Parliamentary Secretary to the Board of Trade (Captain Charles Waterhouse) assured a questioner in the House of Commons that '... there is no evidence to show that the introduction of standard clothing is either necessary or desirable', and that price control powers, taken by the Board of Trade under the Goods and Services (Price Control) Bill in the summer of 1941, were enough to ensure adequate supplies of working-class clothing.[5]

Civil servants, given the Ministerial committee's remit, at first worked on the basis that 'standard' production would be limited to a small range of popular fabrics, cheap, but just sufficiently durable to give good service. As we have seen, the effect of clothes rationing had been to encourage the public to go for maximum quality per coupon. Makers-up and distributors had a vested interest in encouraging the consumer to choose higher quality, higher priced items. Clothing prices continued to rise; the clothing component of the cost-of-living index had reached 175 in May 1941, well ahead of other items. The trend had been accentuated by the application of Purchase Tax from October 1940; the official index may well have underestimated the real increase.

Although the EP(M) discussion had envisaged a scheme being in place by the autumn of 1940, preparation took more than a year. To underpin both rationing and the proposed 'standard' scheme, civil servants put together a national clothing 'budget' – an estimate of the number of garments likely to be bought each year, divided between 'standard' (what became Utility) cloths and the rest. The Board of Trade made a working assumption that 'standard' clothing should meet the demands of all adults and children in households with a family income below £200 a year, plus 25 per cent of adults and 50 per cent of children in households with £200-£300 a year. Later, once the Utility scheme was further developed, it was hoped that it would represent 75–80 per cent of all cloth for garments. Although it might have seemed attractive to aim for 100 per cent (which would have maximized both productivity and quality), in practice this could not be done: not all raw material was suitable for Utility specifications and not all firms had machinery or labour suitable for mass production. The percentages fluctuated year by year, but were always much higher for cotton and rayon cloths than for wool, as Table 2.1 (below) shows in respect of two periods during the war (detail on deliveries of Utility and non-Utility cloths throughout the war can be found in the volume of the official history by Hargreaves and Gowing):

Table 2.1   Deliveries of woven cloth for clothing (million sq. yds.)

	Wool		Cotton		Rayon	
	Utility	non-Utility	Utility	non-Utility	Utility	non-Utility
Aug.–Dec. 1942	146	37	234	62	124	26
Sept.–Oct. 1945	157	30	226	53	127	34

(Source: PRO, BT 131/37.)

Having worked out the total 'budget', Board of Trade civil servants had two major tasks: to draw up the specifications for what would become Utility cloth and garments, and to devise ways to stimulate Utility production and restrain non-Utility. An initial attempt at that second task was a new Woven Textiles (Cloth and Apparel) Order (*S.R. & O. 1941 No. 1281*) in August 1941 which extended the existing raw materials quota controls for a further nine months, but with the added refinement of a larger quota for Utility than for non-Utility. For practical purposes, however, that supposed inducement was meaningless; neither raw materials nor the national total of clothing coupons available would have allowed manufacturers to produce up to the limit, even if they had wanted to. Eventually, the policy of 'designating' firms for Utility production, which is described later in this chapter, gave a stronger degree of control.

The early summer saw a number of more practical moves towards the Utility scheme. The first Director General of Civilian Clothing, Metford Watkins, a director of the John Lewis department stores, was appointed (he was succeeded, three months later, by Sir Thomas

Barlow, who held the position for the rest of the war). Next, and confusingly, the Government announced, in July, what it called the Essential Clothing Programme, which aimed to relieve the current shortages of children's and 'working class' clothing by allowing manufacturers to exceed their quotas of cloth in return for promises to produce loosely defined 'essential' items. Unfortunately, work on allocating cloth to makers-up and on defining and pricing 'Essential' clothing then went forward at the same time as the final discussions about specifications for what would emerge as Utility cloths; not surprisingly, few manufacturers or retailers ever fully understood the difference between the two programmes, while consumers were scarcely aware of the 'Essential' programme at all before it was overtaken by Utility.

More productively the Board of Trade announced that the British Standards Institution (BSI) would take charge of producing detailed specifications for what were still being termed 'standard' cloths. The BSI in fact already had a committee, set up at the end of 1940, to establish standards for goods of various kinds, representing the Institution's first move into the field of consumer protection. By autumn 1941 BSI had set up a number of sub-committees, each covering a type of cloth, which called in evidence and proposals from trade associations and from individual manufacturers and retailers. Among those who advised BSI and the Board of Trade was Marks and Spencer which, in the mid-1930s, had set up its own laboratories and a merchandise development department which worked with suppliers on detailed specifications for cloth and garments.[6]

The advice of the trade and the need to cater for a variety of customers' needs had to be weighed against the wish of Ministers to finalize a practical scheme and get goods into the shops during the autumn of 1941 (advertisements for women's Utility clothes started to appear in the trade press in October). Inevitably, therefore, the first cloth specifications were rough and ready, offering the customer little guarantee of quality; the Order which gave effect to the new scheme merely identified the name, number and ceiling price of 40 cloths, 16 of them cotton. Individual manufacturers were left free to choose their own patterns and designs, so long as they kept to the fabric types in the specifications. Neither then nor later was it intended to draw up Utility specifications for garments themselves – except for overalls (where standardization was virtually complete) and women's underwear: Utility clothes were simply those made from Utility cloth; it was the style or 'austerity' regulations (discussed in the previous Chapter) which constrained design and construction of both Utility and non-Utility clothing.

All of this minimized the risk of the Government being pilloried for 'standardization'. Unfortunately, some of the cloth produced to meet the initial loose specifications hurriedly put in place in 1941 would give Utility a bad name; at this stage the scheme seemed little more than a convenient label for the varieties of cotton cloths normally consumed by lower-income groups. Manufacturers and distributors, despite the care taken by the Board of Trade to consult the industry bodies, disliked the low prices and profit margins on Utility products, gave their production a lower priority and, according to BoT officials, did not always give the care and attention to the cut and finish of Utility goods that they gave to their other products.[7]

By this time the name Utility had finally been revealed not only to the trade but to the public; its identifying feature appeared in November when the Order (*S.R. & O. 1941 No. 1614*) was issued forcing manufacturers to apply to Utility cloths, and to garments made from them, the unique Utility mark (see illustration, Plate 8). On 21 January 1942 the President of the Board of Trade (at that time Sir Andrew Duncan) was able to tell the House of Commons that men's Utility suits, complete with Utility label, were beginning to appear in the shops, although not in any quantity; women's suits, dresses, skirts and coats had been arriving in selected shops since the turn of the year. The consolidating Order (*Utility Apparel (Maximum Prices and Charges) Order*), which brought together all of the provisions concerning Utility prices and margins, came into effect on 4 February.

Publicly, the Board of Trade said that the 'CC 41' mark had 'no special significance apart from the figures indicating the date of its first use'. It is easy enough to work out, however, that the letters CC derived from 'civilian clothing'; later use of the identical mark for other Utility goods including furniture and household textiles was convenient, if illogical (logic, like truth, is doubtless an early casualty in all wars). The designer, Reginald Shipp, was said to have been instructed to design the double C 'so that the public should not recognise the letters as such'.[8] Later, in 1943, a further Order (*S.R. & O. 1943 No. 1208*) required clothes to carry not only the Utility mark itself, but also the specification number of the cloth; that refinement was unsuccessfully resisted by some in the trade.

The Board of Trade's machinery for monitoring and enforcing the Utility rules was limited; in the end, manufacturers risked a penalty only if a dissatisfied customer complained, for example to his or her local Price Regulation Committee. Nevertheless, when the Douglas Committee (see Chapter 5) reviewed the history of Utility, in 1951, it believed that there had been at least a 'satisfactory' observance of the rules, since traders and manufacturers were sufficiently afraid of being reported, losing cloth allocations or even being put out of business. All in all, however, the Board of Trade may have been somewhat bold when it claimed, in briefing the media in 1944, that:

> 'The Utility mark is ... a guarantee to the public ... which has become the widest known official "trade mark" ever introduced'.[9]

(See pages 100–101 for discussion of the effect on this claim of changes later made to the quality guarantee element of Utility, and the extent to which Utility may have been a precursor of present day labelling systems.)

The first Utility schedule, having specified the relatively small number of cloths, gave a brief description of each of them, their width and, for some of the wool cloths, the minimum weight. The schedule also listed the kind of garments into which each cloth could be made up and the maximum price at which it might be sold. Indeed, at this stage it was the simplification of price control – something which cloth quotas, rationing and the Essential Clothing Scheme had been unable to achieve – which was seen by officials as the main benefit of Utility. During final discussions with the trade, in early autumn 1941, officials found that at least one major manufacturer, Wolsey, expected to have no difficulty selling Utility clothing well within the ceiling prices, and estimated that the maximum Utility prices for men's suits, overcoats and raincoats would be 6–7 per cent less than prices in the 'normal market'.[10]

Two months later the list of Utility cloths was extended and, in some cases, minimum as well as maximum manufacturers' prices were specified. The schedule to the new Order set out the sizes, quality and maximum price for underwear and knitwear which could be described as Utility. Later Orders added other garments to the list. Separate Orders refined and extended the system of price control; maximum prices charged by the manufacturer should not exceed costs of 'production and sale' plus a percentage mark-up varying between 4 and 7.5 per cent according to the class of garment (wholesale and retail margins were fixed at 20 per cent and 33.3 per cent respectively). The Orders listed items which could legitimately count towards manufacturers' costs.

More detailed specifications took effect in June 1942, produced under the aegis of the BSI after further consultation with manufacturers; the final list still included the original rough and ready type and price definitions for woollen cloth, but much more precise specifications were now provided for cotton and rayon. To the trade, the woollen specifications were known as 'three figure', the later cotton and rayon specifications as 'four figure' definitions,[11] many of which survived in common use until well after the war. Later in the war a whole new range of better quality cloths was added, after pressure from the trade, for making up into more expensive Utility garments, so expanding the market for Utility considerably.

At the same time changes were made to the allocation of materials. By June 1942 the original Limitations of Supply Orders were suspended. Makers-up of garments had to work out their estimated production on the basis of orders received from distributors, who had to 'pay' for supplies in both ordinary and coupon currency. The estimates were passed on to the Board of Trade's Clothing Control which then decided the exact yardage of Utility cloth to allocate to each firm. Total output was not shared evenly among all manufacturers. One of the central aims of Utility was to reduce costs of production in the clothing industry as a whole by encouraging makers-up to undertake long runs on a smaller range of garments. To do this the Board of Trade tried to identify firms best able to produce Utility goods economically. Such firms would then be 'designated'. Designated firms agreed to devote not less than 75 per cent of their production capacity either to Utility clothing, to other Government contract work (for example, service uniforms) or to exports; they would in turn receive at least 65 per cent of the available Utility yardage.

As well as benefiting from – more or less – guaranteed allocations of raw materials, the Ministry of Labour agreed that firms designated for Utility clothing production would be scheduled under the Essential Works Order and would have reasonable security of labour. This protection seems not always to have worked; in May 1942 Board of Trade officials noted that there was a decided 'drift' of labour from designated firms, alleging that the Ministry of Labour was interviewing the women and 'unsettling them' (by suggesting, deliberately or not, that they might be directed to other work).[12]

In November 1941 it was estimated that total labour in the industry was around 565,000, but that the 66-coupon clothing ration might need no more than 198,000 workers. The task of identifying firms to be designated started by taking a census of the 3,000 firms in the clothing industry which had more than 50 employees. Smaller firms were, however, also invited to come forward. Those known to produce clothes in or around the new Utility price range were first choice, unless the Ministry of Labour objected. The Admiralty, Ministry of Supply and Ministry of Transport also had to be consulted, as did a dozen trade associations, trades unions and chambers of commerce. The Board of Trade had to consider not only facts about the firm itself – its factory space, machinery, product range and labour – but also the local labour situation and especially local demand for labour in munitions factories.

By mid-December 1941 about 600 factories had been designated, with 91,000 employees, 58,000 of whom the Board of Trade thought would be engaged on Utility production, the remainder on exports and other non-Utility. By March 1942 employment in designated firms was nearing 130,000 and about 60 per cent of wool cloth was allocated to them. Designated firms tended to be larger than average; only 7 per cent of them had fewer than 20 employees, compared with 36 per cent in the industry as a whole in 1939. Non-designated factories could continue in production – provided they could get the raw materials. Designation was therefore not identical to the concentration of industry, described in Chapter 1. Theoretically the two should have been complementary, but in practice they did not always sit happily together; the Overall Manufacturers Association (OMA) believed that 'designation was the most difficult problem the trade had to face'.[13]

The relationship between concentration and designation for Utility did give constant trouble. Although concentration may have left the total size of the industry (measured by number of factories) roughly equivalent to the total capacity envisaged in the Board of Trade's 'budget', it had not, unfortunately, always left intact those plants potentially most efficient in producing Utility clothes – that is, those best suited to long runs of relatively simple mass-produced garments. Once the skilled labour of a non-nucleus factory had been dispersed, it could not be called back; thus the Board of Trade had to do its best in terms of the existing structure of the industry.

In a letter to the Board of Trade in March 1944 the Secretary of the Wholesale Fashion Trades Association (Maurice Tuke) revealed understandable irritation and confusion regarding the two schemes. The BoT's ruling that firms making up non-Utility women's clothing would most likely not be considered for 'nucleus' status under concentration 'caused great perturbation throughout the fashion industry of London', he said. But the Board had its own priorities; non-nucleus firms could not expect to keep more employees than were required for Government work and the essential needs of the civilian population.[14]

Problems were particularly pronounced in the hosiery sector where, in any case, Board of Trade officials admitted that their initial estimates of the volume of yarn that would be needed for interlock hosiery had been much too low.[15] Although concentration had left the sector at roughly the right size to meet the capacity identified in the BoT's 'budget', it had not always preserved the most efficient producers of Utility lines. The Directorate of Civilian Hosiery (the 'Hosiery Control') had to intervene directly, allocating yarn to individual firms to make those garments for which their machinery and labour force were best suited. In fact, under this direct control, Utility achieved a higher proportion of all hosiery production – 96 per cent – than of any other type of garment except overalls.

In Whitehall and the provincial centres where the Wool and Cotton Controls operated, officials fought to get higher proportions of raw materials allocated to designated firms. In the case of wool cloth, for example, the Board of Trade received constant complaints from designated companies that supplies were going to undesignated competitors. The official history confirms that undesignated firms did indeed receive more cloth.[16] The understanding between the BoT and Wool Control was foundering because of the latter's reluctance to intervene in the affairs of individual cloth manufacturers, many of whom tended, naturally enough, to favour old customers, whether they were designated or not. Eventually, after experimenting with licences, the BoT itself intervened with a system of 'key certificates', issued to designated firms for wool or cotton cloth and based upon needs estimated by the Board's own clothing 'budget'.

From its initial stand-off position, the Board of Trade had steadily become more deeply involved in the mechanics of clothing production. In some cases the Board had to face competition from the Ministry of Supply for supplies of cloth (and of leather for boots and shoes). When, in 1942, it appeared that supplies of cotton cloth for Utility clothing would not be enough to meet the Board's estimated 'budget', Hugh Dalton (President of the Board of Trade from 1942–45) appealed to his Ministerial colleagues to cut back the apparently insatiable demand of the armed services for men's underwear, pointing out that if civilians were left with clothing coupons for which there were no goods in the shops, morale would suffer and the Utility scheme be discredited.

One final and essential element of the Utility scheme remained to be put in place. In August 1942 an Order (*Purchase Tax (Exemptions)(No. 4) Order, S. R. & O. 1942 No. 1506*) was made exempting virtually all Utility goods from Purchase Tax; only garments made entirely from fur materials and fully-fashioned stockings continued to attract tax. Treasury officials, unsurprisingly, argued strongly from 1941 onwards against this concession. When, during that summer of 1942, Utility furniture was introduced and household textiles added to the clothing scheme, Dalton claimed that he had persuaded Kingsley Wood to disregard the advice of his officials, provided that Dalton promised no further additions to the Utility product range.[17] Next year, however, the Treasury was still worrying about the number of 'miscellaneous items' being included in the Utility scheme and the consequent loss of revenue. A Board of Trade minute (21 April 1943) admitted that logic had not always prevailed; the range of Utility cloths and apparel had grown as a consequence of 'a series of biological urges rather than as an orderly sequence pre-determined in the light of a master plan'.[18]

Despite a general antipathy to regulation and the specific problems caused by concentration and designation, many manufacturers had by then come to see the value of the Utility scheme: it could increase their chances of getting raw materials and also offer them a fixed profit on a fixed price item with a long production run. The ribbon manufacturers, for example, pressed unsuccessfully for Utility ribbons; hatters were equally unlucky (perhaps because, as we have seen, Hugh Dalton was unsympathetic). Board of Trade civil servants were divided among themselves about the merits of some of the ideas for additional items: a senior official quoted Utility umbrellas as a particularly dubious idea, adding sternly that IM officials could not be expected to be 'constantly running round to Great George Street [the Treasury] each time some of us feel that it would be a good thing if we had Utility ribbons, counterpanes or what have you'.[19] Inter-Departmental struggles between Board of Trade and Treasury over Purchase Tax exemption became a central feature of post-war debate about whether or not Utility should continue; among the public that debate would reach its most emotive level in relation to silk and nylon stockings.

By the summer of 1942, therefore, the final shape of the Utility scheme was complete: specifications for cloth; fixed prices and profits; specified types of clothing; designated manufacturers; guaranteed quality; preference for Utility over non-Utility in terms of raw materials and tax. Just as important as these production elements was the Board of Trade's marketing or public relations role. Every effort was made to steer the media and the public away from the term 'standard', which civil servants knew would bring thunder down on them from both Fleet Street and Downing Street. 'Does Utility mean standardisation?' was a question asked the BoT's annual 'Clothing Quiz'. The response was firm:

'No: the object of the Utility scheme is not to standardise but to ensure the best possible use is made of supplies. The Board of Trade had no wish to adopt the role of fashion dictator; manufacturers could create their own designs, provided that they conformed to Utility specifications and were satisfactory as regards fitting and durability'.[20]

Public suspicion of 'standardization', although understandable, was to a large extent unfounded; whatever Ministers preferred it would have been difficult to enforce standardization on an industry as scattered, fragmented and disparate as garment-making. The eventual Utility Orders for cotton and rayon cloth, although rigid by comparison with their predecessors (and with those for woollen cloths), laid down specifications only for construction, not colour or design; the resultant variations in finish were enough to conceal any trace of standardization from the ultimate customer. In 1943 a Utility Fabric Exhibition at the Cotton Board's Colour, Design and Style Centre in Manchester was able to show over 2,000 different samples, ranging from 1/4 (7p) to 3/- (15p) per yard for cotton, and from 2/- (10p) to 6/- (30p) per yard for rayon, produced from 160 different Utility specifications. Many attributes, such as crease-resistant finishes, which we now take for granted, were given widespread publicity as part of Utility specifications; 'Clothes that look Pricey are often Utility', pointed out an advertisement in the *Drapers' Record* (November 1942).

In February 1942 the now forgotten Andrew Duncan had, with a fleeting interregnum under Col. J. J. Llewellin, given way to Dalton, the first of three noted Labour politicians and Utility enthusiasts at the Board of Trade.[21] Dalton became enduringly identified with austerity and Utility; it was he who took credit for the Board of Trade's decision to invite ten leading fashion designers, members of the Incorporated Society of London Fashion Designers (ISLFD),[22] to prepare designs for women's coats, dresses, blouses and skirts, for Utility production. The ISLFD stemmed from the pre-war Fashion Group of London. After the fall of France, and the arrival in London of refugee Paris designers, a new constitution was drawn up. The Board of Trade encouraged the new group from the outset, in the interests of an export drive; for their part the designers saw the advantages of presenting a common front when dealing with Board of Trade and other bureaucrats.

In the late summer of 1942 there took place a series of trade showings of the ISLFD's initial designs (the original models went to the Victoria and Albert Museum as a record of the first 'Government commissioned clothes'). Templates, like architects' blueprints, were made, and offered to manufacturers for nominal fees 'as an indication of how ... Utility clothes may be produced with charm and variety', said the Ministry of Information press notice. After the trade show over 100 manufacturers placed orders for them, although the *Drapers' Record* (October, 1942) pointed out that there were only eight designs each for women's suits, coats, dresses and blouses, and that they would be in the shops too late for the main autumn selling season. The journal also suggested that any supposed glamour added by the ISLFD designers' names might not last long.

More charitably, *Vogue* (June 1942) congratulated the BoT on 'very intelligently' asking for designs 'with the clean elegance of a style stripped of all superfluities', concentrating on 'fundamental qualities – boldness or subtlety of colour schemes ... superb cut ... fabrics in interesting weaves. Not a fashion revolution, but a narrowing of the fashion field, well suited to these times'. The *Vogue* sub-heading 'Dress restraint – yes; Fashion restriction – no!' helpfully endorsed the 'no standardization' line with which Board of Trade and Ministry of Information press officers fed the media.

The couturiers' designs had, of course, not only to use Utility specification cloth, but conform to 'austerity' style rules. Hardy Amies, who in 1941–1942 was an officer in the Intelligence Corps moonlighting as a designer for the House of Worth, writes in his memoirs that: 'Curiously enough I hardly found those regulations irksome. I had settled down to an extreme sobriety of design' which 'fitted well into the schemes for Utility clothing'.[23] Another ISLFD member, Digby Morton, had been interviewed by Mass Observation in March 1942. He complained about the amount of paperwork and bureaucracy in dealing with BoT and other departments ('You have to fight like hell to get anything, and you're always having to write about something ... getting this, that and the other') and about the unrealistic timetable the designers had been given. He could see that many shops would not like Utility 'because of their profits', but as a designer he was firmly in favour; like Amies, he approved the simple dresses, 'rather tailored and plain', which resulted from the match of Utility and austerity.[24]

One could hardly expect the official view of Utility, for example as expressed in Board of Trade press notices, to have been anything other than enthusiastic. The recollection of professionals – designers and fashion trade press – provide rather more objective support for the view that, overall, Utility clothes were, if not exciting, at worst tolerable and arguably part of the mainstream of English design.

NOTES

1   Laver, 1979, p230.

2   For example, in the journal of George Beardmore, later published as *Civilians at War* (OUP, 1986), the term 'pool', meaning un-branded, was officially applied to petrol but its use for clothes was less common. At least one manufacturer did produce a prototype civilian 'uniform' (see Plate 4).

3   EP(M)(40)9, in PRO, CAB 72/3.

4   PRO, BT 64/76; apart from the Utility scheme, the same branch of the IM Department dealt with questions about the allocation of raw materials, labour, coupons, prohibition of metal toys, special licences for supplementary supplies of gramophone records and needles. The Branch's post-bag averaged 36,000 letters a month, 40 of them for Ministerial reply.

5   HofC, Vol. 373, Col. 619.

6   Rees, 1973, p162, and interview with M&S consultant, 1993. Marks and Spencer was unusual in having this kind of scientific department; work on technical specifications was at first led by Erich Kann, a scientist employed by a German department store before seeking refuge in Britain; Selfridges was thought to be the only other major British store with a similar facility. The close relationship on quality control between M&S and the manufacturers Corah, of Leicester, was also unusual at that time.

7   PRO, BT 131/35.

8   Idris Cleaver in *The Woodworker*, June 1983; the same source claims that it was Alison McInnes, secretary to Sir Laurence Watkinson at the BoT, who hit upon the term Utility; if so, she should have been better rewarded and remembered.

9   MoI brief R539, 21 Dec. 1944; official records make it clear that in most Utility schemes enforcement depended entirely on complaints being received from the public, then followed up with manufacturers – usually by way of technical experts, for example in the Cotton Board and the Shirley Institute. In a handful of cases BoT threatened to take away the manufacturer's right to use the Utility mark, at least temporarily. In the case of furniture and footwear (see Chapter 4), technical officers were employed to visit factories (BT 64/735).

10 PRO, BT64/182.

11 *Drapers' Record*, Feb. 1942.

12 PRO, BT 64/861.

13 Warwick, MSS 222; OMA annual reports are models of clarity, information and neat presentation.
14 PRO, BT 64/861; less restrained than Maurice Tuke was the writer of an earlier letter to *The Times* (16 June 1942) who accused the BoT of ruthlessly scrapping the 'established delicate and complex machinery of production and distribution' in favour of 'chaos and bewilderment'.
15 Hargreaves and Gowing, 1951, pp460–461.
16 Ibid.
17 Dalton, 1986, p406; Dalton boasted that he and Kingsley Wood were 'two of a rather small number of Ministers who understood a deal'.
18 PRO, BT 64/139.
19 Ibid.
20 *Clothing Quiz*, HMSO, Nov. 1943 (see Plate 8).
21 Stafford Cripps and Harold Wilson were the others; in 1942 Wilson was a junior temporary civil servant in the BoT's Mines Department and Hugh Gaitskell, another future Labour leader, was Dalton's Principal Private Secretary, later personal assistant.
22 Members included Hardy Amies, Norman Hartnell, Peter Russell, Worth, Bianca Mosca, Angele Delanghe, Digby Morton, Victor Stiebel, Molyneux, Charles Creed, Michael Sherard, plus representatives of the wholesale trade; see Laver, 1979, p253.
23 Amies, 1984, p40.
24 M-OA, Topic collection 4/E.

CHAPTER 3

'They're beauties ... They're Utilities': Press and Public Reaction to Utility Clothes

'The first Utility I've seen. Shocking stuff. It's like sacking.'
Mass Observation interviewee, March 1942

In general, the Utility tailored suits and topcoats for women which the ISLFD members launched in 1942 got a positive reaction from fashion writers at the time and from fashion historians subsequently. They could hardly be said to be innovative; their merit lay in opening up English classic design to the wartime mass market: 'As these were the garments in which English makers had always excelled, the workers looked far better dressed ... while the moneyed women looked much as they had always done in the open air', writes Alison Settle.[1]

Fashion writers have given less attention to Utility suits for men. The combination of Utility cloth and austerity restrictions resulted in suits in familiar materials but with slightly shorter jackets, lacking waist pleats, breast pocket or buttons on the cuffs. Buckles disappeared from waistcoats and trousers. Trousers narrowed slightly and, of course, had no turn-ups. Apart from that last deprivation, the average male customer would probably have found it difficult to spot significant differences between Utility suits and the styles which preceded them. There was a gratifying impact on price; the Central Price Regulation Committee (CPRC) suggested that maximum prices for men's Utility suits, overcoats and raincoats were around 6–7 per cent less than those in the 'normal market'.

Having announced the name and the essential elements of the Utility scheme, the Board of Trade got initial reactions from retailers. During the autumn and winter of 1941–1942 the keynote was confusion, not least between the short-lived 'Essential Clothing' scheme and Utility. Initial reports suggested that in spite of official publicity in the trade press, 'Utility is still much of a mystery to most tailors and outfitters'.[2] Some shopkeepers made sure customers were further confused by applying the word Utility extensively to all kinds of unrationed articles such as handbags and tablecloths, outside the Utility range. Officials were pessimistic:

> 'The public's reaction to the word Utility is one of great disinterest, if not complete indifference as far as fabrics are concerned. Ordinary merchandise is bought freely but they shy off anything marked Utility.'

By February 1942, however, when the national press was starting to give serious coverage to Utility, the Drapers' Chamber of Trade was able to send BoT officials a more cheerful report: those shops which had received Utility clothes thought the quality good; in South Wales, for unexplained reasons, 'the reception ... has been remarkably enthusiastic'. Some retailers thought that, although good quality, certain Utility lines were too high in price, quoting crepe or satin women's underwear at 9/3 (46p) a set as an example; poplin was thought to be a more appropriate material. A few retailers were still saying that they would not touch any Utility goods until all other types ceased to be available. A particular problem in the early days was that different manufacturers could produce cloth bearing the same Utility specification number at different prices, because the costs on which they based the selling price were different. The changes to specifications introduced later in 1942 (noted in Chapter 2) would help eliminate this anomaly.

It was clear from the outset that the larger stores would be more enthusiastic. Owen Owen and T J Hughes, both of Liverpool, stated that Utility was generally considered to be 'extremely good value'; their main problem (February 1942) was the slow pace of deliveries. Six months later a Board of Trade trawl among its correspondents found that the chain stores, including Marks and Spencer, tended to sell nearly all Utility goods well below the maximum prices, but in the department stores and smaller shops practice varied widely; a high proportion of the Kensington trade was below the maximum price, but in the West End (where costs were higher) most Utility clothes were sold for the ceiling price.

As early as October 1941, when Utility supplies were only trickling into the shops, the *Drapers' Record* had found some large London stores starting to promote Utility with window displays. An executive at D. H. Evans, in the West End, confirmed that 'We shall go out for it [Utility] 100%'. But the journal, with an eye to its main readership, also repeatedly warned of the danger that small shops would be forced out of business: Utility profit margins were too slender to allow them to compete with the chain stores (although an editorial pointed out that on the whole it was better to have price controlled, Utility stock to sell than none at all). In particular, small dress shops would not be able to take Utility cloth, make it up to customers' own orders and still remain within the ceiling price. Small traders were also said to be appalled by the complexity of the paperwork: 'The whole scheme ... appears very unwieldy and complicated. Time alone will show whether these faults render it unworkable'. It was a mystery how the Board of Trade had worked out the maximum prices, the first draft of which, in September 1941, had run to 25 closely typed foolscap pages, with a further 17 pages for hosiery.

Drapers' Record's fashion correspondent, however, was not displeased with the designs themselves: 'There is plenty of room for high class manufacturers, many of whom will say "Let's give them the best we can"'. Although she characterized the ISLFD designs as 'rougher, more colourful altogether, [with] more rustic varieties' than pre-Utility styles, she thought them 'well marked for general town popularity'.

In February 1942, Mass Observation produced the first of several reports on Utility clothes[3] which edited together comments of shop assistants, customers and window shoppers in and around London stores. A display of Utility suits and dresses at D. H. Evans was described, and a shop assistant interviewed. Already selling well were Utility frocks at prices between 15/- (75p) and 47/11 (£2.39), and plain styled check coats – 'Classic styles, with tie in front and large pockets' – at 55/6 to 79/6 (£2.78 to £3.97).

A shop assistant thought that these first Utility clothes were:

'... lovely – now ... the next lot won't be. You see they have still got some of the old nice materials, but after this they won't be anything like so nice. I suppose it's a good idea these Utility things. They're good for the money – now.'

The manageress of a 'fairly large Edgware Road shop' was more blunt:

'It's bloody awful. There's no one in the shop. People don't like the cloth. Women know that for £4 or so you can't get a really good coat. The dresses are very pretty. The style and colour are good. That's the only way we can sell the tripe.'

By the end of March, Mass Observation observers had spotted large stocks of Utility dresses, coats and suits in all the popular stores. A branch of Richard Shops reported 75 per cent of its stock as being Utility, but the manager added that his assistants did not use the word unless customers mentioned it first. Window displays, again avoiding the term Utility, enabled the MO reporter to count the proportion of window shoppers ('67% of women glancing at display in Peter Robinson stopped to look at them closer'), the time they spent ('varying from 2 to 10 seconds and sometimes up to a couple of minutes', generally longer than they devoted to the more expensive, non-Utility windows), and to note favourable comments on simple, well-designed styles in green tweed suits, pastel pink and blue, scarlet or green dresses, and classic tweed coats in plaid and check designs.

'A few' unfavourable comments were noted about the coarseness ('like sacking') of material in the 'finer' (i.e. lighter weight, lower quality) wool dresses, coats and suits; one customer, echoing the views of the shopworkers reported earlier, believed that: 'Utility clothes would go shabby with six months hard wear'.

Most customers, however, seemed to find the clothes surprisingly good but disliked the name Utility:

'I expected them all to be the same, but there's quite a wide range of styles, and the materials are good' (20-year old woman customer);

'They look very well cut, and certainly reasonably priced. It [Utility] justifies itself on the strength that it brings the price of clothes to suit everybody's purse' (unidentified interviewee).

Mass Observation pointed out that many people who commented unfavourably on Utility in the first half of 1942 were doing so without having seen the clothes. Men were particularly prone to do this; the relatively small number of male MO interviewees who spoke against the scheme had not then seen any of the clothes. But as stocks and window displays increased, so the proportion 'definitely in favour' grew to over 60 per cent; the proportion 'definitely against' fell from 18 per cent to 9 per cent. The Mass Observation reporter's conclusion was that 'In spite of the irritation and apprehension caused by the past publicity and propaganda, people are fairly well disposed to accept this latest form of conscription – the conscription of fashion'. She went on to deduce, correctly, the reason why the scheme was likely to be so unpopular with the small shopkeeper:

'... the Utility scheme is quite acceptable to large chain stores with a guaranteed turnover and regular trade. They can interchange goods between branches, and are sufficiently organised and financed to sell Utility clothes in bulk and make a margin of profit which allows them to run. Smaller dress shops, however, ... are in danger of either concentrating on uncontrolled, higher priced goods in order to maintain overheads, or to close down.'

J. M. Paynton, of the Drapers' Chamber of Trade, confirmed that:

'... the retailers are against it for the simple reason that it doesn't allow them margin for profit ... they lose money on every Utility garment they sell. Then people are saying, when shown a Utility garment, "Haven't you anything *better*?". That's the result of press publicity and emphasis on *standard* clothes. The next stage is where they begin to realise that Utility isn't so bad after all ... in a year to eighteen months, I forecast everything will be on a Utility margin and the higher-priced clothes will have to come down to the level of Utility. The public will refuse to buy them otherwise.'

More comprehensive, although perhaps less colourful, than Mass Observation's essays were the Ministry of Information's Home Intelligence Reports. Circulated around Whitehall, each month they included a list of 'constant topics' – subjects which a high proportion of MoI informants found recurring among their contacts. Between June 1943 and April 1944 the poor quality and/or cost of Utility clothes featured regularly on that list, with up to seven separate sources quoted in one week. However, the subject was only ever covered by a minority of MoI's sources – typically seven out of the 30 or so used each month – and the complaints were usually about particular garments rather than Utility in general. Apart from hosiery, the most common complaints concerned the poor quality and high coupon value of children's Utility clothes.

Some reports suggested that the Board of Trade should somehow enforce a switch of manufacturing resources from 'fancy gowns' to 'hard wearing Utility shorts' for boys; a Birmingham headmaster wrote to the *Daily Telegraph* (21 March 1942) on the same theme, arguing that boys should be forced to wear shorts, not 'long, greasy, unpressed flannel bags'. Complaints about the lack of larger-size women's clothes and corsets appeared in a couple of monthly reports. Interestingly it was suggested (report of 1 April 1943) that, in addition to the Utility mark and cloth specification number, Utility clothes should be identified with a serial number so that faulty goods could be checked back to the garment maker.

The reports contain far fewer complaints specific to men's clothes than to women's or children's. One report stands out, in April 1943, although it provided little substantiation and characteristically lumped Utility together with style restrictions, including the ban on trouser turn-ups:

> 'Men's Utility suits are said to be thoroughly disliked in the North Midlands Region. Utility shirts are skimpy and cut so they half strangle you.'[4]

Leading authors of the day found themselves divided on this issue. Introducing his novel *Three Men in New Suits* (Heinemann, 1945), J. B. Priestley thought it necessary to apologize for having written, mistakenly, that demobilized soldiers were to receive the Utility suits 'that had been so unpopular with civilians'; having inspected the civilian 'demob' outfits he was reassured to find them of 'excellent quality'. On the other hand the much-loved essayist Robert Lynd, writing in the *News Chronicle* (7 March 1942), was more complaisant:

> 'Make Utility clothes the fashion and all the male sex, with the exception of a few Irish eccentrics like the Duke of Wellington and Mr Shaw, will love them. The truth is, men do not care about clothes.'

In March 1942 Mass Observation also interviewed Ann Seymour, the editress (*sic*) of *Woman & Beauty*:

'The only thing wrong with [Utility] is the name. They're really very good ... but they haven't been put over properly. I should be quite pleased to buy them. I should buy something one size too big for me ... and then take it to my tailor and let him make it fit me for a guinea or two. This scheme is all to the good if it allows poor people to buy clothes that are going to last; as it is [i.e. pre-Utility] they can't afford to, and have to spend all their coupons buying shoddy boots and coats. People have been constantly ringing up to ask where they can get the suit [illustrated in *Woman & Beauty*] ... the distribution's so bad. The assistants are to blame quite a lot ... they haven't been given any sales talk. They don't take much trouble or interest over it. The Government should have launched a proper campaign. The word Utility is awful. The designers must be built up, that seems to me the most important thing.'[5]

In the popular press as a whole, there was steady coverage of the women's Utility designs; approval of the clothes themselves but distaste for the name Utility was the common theme in the first months of 1942. 'Women fight shy of "Utility" Clothes' was a typical (*Sunday Chronicle*, 22 February 1942) headline, the journalist alleging that women had been scared off by the 'bleak description which gives no idea of the exciting range of clothes', and so were missing 'some of the best bargains of their lives'. Shops found the name Utility so lacking in sales appeal that they preferred to label the goods 'Government control priced'. Shoppers were said to believe that Utility meant a 'shapeless, hardwearing garment for workers'.

Daily Mirror journalist Kathleen Pearcey (16 March 1942) wrote with admiration and excitement about 'First rate styles. ... Utility coats get full marks for cut, material and finish! Utility glamour may sound impossible, but ... the authorities have used their imaginations!' Readers, she believed, would wear Utility clothes not because they were patriotic but because Utility was the best value on the market in terms of price and hard-wearing quality. The article concluded firmly: 'There is nothing dull or depressed about Utility clothes'.

Writing for what would in normal times have been a different segment of the market, *The Times*, on the launch of Utility, had been characteristically cautious: 'The cloth for coats appeared to be in a good range of colour' was the verdict on a showing to women journalists in November 1941, but a coat and skirt, priced at 97/- (£4.85), was 'not very attractive'. Once goods had started to appear in the shops, however, the tone became warmer: 'the utility of clothing has long been too generally subordinated to its power of adornment', suggested a fourth leader in March 1942, praising the Director General of Civilian Clothing for striking a blow at 'an error which may go back to the gates of the Garden of Eden'. The writer credited the Director General, Sir Thomas Barlow, with saying that there had been 'a most unreasonable use of colour in normal times', which Utility would correct – a view rather at odds with the official line that choice of colour and design was unaffected by Utility. The leader writer, presumably a man, shied away from venturing any opinion on the length of skirts, but, like Robert Lynd, thought that Utility and austerity would 'give men a good opportunity of keeping up the old pretence that they do not care what they wear', and came out firmly on the Dalton, anti-turn-up, side.

By September 1942, when Simpson's (Piccadilly) put on a show of winter Utility designs, *The Times* had been won over completely. Under the headline '"Utility", but Smart' it wrote that the show would:

'do much to remove a lingering idea that Utility clothes must necessarily be standardised. ... Fine wool blouses and well cut skirts as well as useful slacks complete a wardrobe which with the removal of the purchase tax from Utility clothes can have the good taste and appearance of models previously costing four times as much.'

When coupons were exhausted, *The Times* added, Simpson's remodelling service would 'transform a man's unwanted tweed overcoat into a woman's sports type of coat, or turn out something smart from a man's town overcoat'.

Some of the improved tone of press reports could be attributed to the fact that, by the summer of 1942, the distribution problems and lack of enthusiasm among shop assistants noted by Mass Observation were less marked. More designs appeared for the press to review. *Vogue* featured Utility designs under the headline 'They're Beauties – They're Utilities', showing suits by Jaeger and others with the characteristic boxy look jackets and pleated skirts. The following month's editorial thought the whole Utility scheme a 'great opportunity for the couture' (a tweed suit being illustrated used the Utility 'CC 41' mark as part of its design). In September, patterns were printed for a suit to be tailored in Otterburn tweed and, in October, *Vogue's* 'Choice of the Month' was a Lyndale Utility all-purpose classic tailored suit in beige tweed, overchecked with lime green on sale at Dickins & Jones, 92/10 (£4.64).

The 29 August issue of *Picture Post* ran a two-page feature by Anne Scott-James on 'Austerity Clothes' which first summed up the progress of restriction since the outbreak of war – limitations on materials, Utility and the 'austerity' rules for making up garments. The feature then duly emphasized the Board of Trade line that these were not 'standard' clothes: dressmakers would still have plenty of scope to offer a wide variety. Anne Scott-James's conclusion was that all of the suits and dresses illustrated were 'good ... even by peacetime standards'; quality would get even better as manufacturers concentrated on cut, for example providing a narrow waistline by more attention to fit of shoulders and skirt. Photographs contrasted styles of 1939 with the Utility models, so as to favour the latter; interestingly, later in the war an advertiser (in *Vogue*) would choose to contrast Utility garments, not with those of the 1930s, but with the 'fussy fashions' seen in Regent Street during the First World War.

The press also liked the wide range and vivid colours of women's Utility blouses, some writers helpfully pointing out that a light coloured blouse in an otherwise dark costume could be useful in the black-out. At least one ingenious manufacturer combined economy of material with extra customer appeal by producing blouses in two halves, buttoning over the shoulder and down the sides, so that different fronts could be worn with the same back. Towards the end of the war *Good Housekeeping* featured a Hart Utility blouse in honey coloured wool, with self stiffened collar and cuffs, at 25/- (£1.25) and six coupons, matched with a Dereta skirt in honey and brown check tweed at £4/15/11 (£4.80) and another six coupons.

Whatever the intrinsic merits of the designs, journalists were of course bombarded with material by Board of Trade and Ministry of Information officials (although trade journals continued to suggest that Utility had been poorly promoted in comparison with the strong campaigns run by the Ministry of Food, under Woolton). We should not be too surprised that after some initial hesitation most journalists, whether writing for a popular newspaper or a quality fashion journal, would choose to accentuate the positive side of Utility, both as a boost to morale and to support an industry struggling against difficulties of all sorts. Further, even the most independent-minded journalist in wartime had to give at least half a thought to the risk of reprisals and unofficial censorship: being rude about the official Utility scheme would get the paper a bad name with the authorities on whom the press depended for editorial copy and, increasingly, for advertising revenue.

By October 1942 the *Wartime Trading Bulletin* claimed that Utility coats were selling more quickly than anything else, and nearly all of the newly released Utility ranges were thought to offer good quality to customers. The outstanding exception was hosiery; women's Utility stockings were said to be uncomfortable and to wear badly. Two months later persistent demand was reported for non-Utility stockings. An adverse report in the *News Chronicle* was said to have caused disaffection among customers.

Utility stockings were certainly cheaper than good quality pre-war products; the CPRC thought that one beneficial effect of Utility might be to break the trade's habit of fixing prices at no less than one shilling (5p) increments. In February 1943 five out of eight Board of Trade regional offices thought it worth recording specific complaints about quality of stockings. The official historians admit that stockings were a constant source of complaint, while maintaining that one particular Utility product (specification 731) was so good – 'Probably the best seamless stocking ever produced in Britain' – that manufacturers of cheap stockings were afraid it would put them out of business.[6]

One of the problems, acknowledged by the Director of Civilian Clothing, was that before the war the market had largely been satisfied by the production of rayon stockings, developed by manufacturers on the basis of rapid consumption and quick replacement. This kind of product was hard hit by rationing: many more women had money to buy stockings frequently, but they did not have enough coupons. Production of fully-fashioned stockings was also affected by labour shortages, as skilled male and female workers were conscripted. Sir Thomas Barlow believed that one practical solution was the addition to the range of a fine Egyptian two-fold cotton stocking which, 'although considered by women to be an inadequate substitute for silk', he personally thought both 'durable and reasonably pleasant in appearance'.[7]

The reactions of cloth and clothing manufacturers were less vividly recorded that those of customers and shopkeepers. Manufacturers were more likely to voice a general complaint against the whole paraphernalia of controls on raw materials, quotas, concentration, direction of labour and, above all, form filling. The issue of *Picture Post* which included Anne Scott-James's appreciative feature on Utility clothes also carried an anguished letter from a Birmingham manufacturer about the 'epic conversations through which the nation's money and the manufacturers' time are being wasted by the futile elderly office boys of Whitehall'; he entreated Government to do something before the last form 'breaks our backs and we are all cutting out paper dolls'.

The Overall Manufacturers Association, whose products were subject to the most rigid control of all, complained regularly about being subjected to large numbers of complicated controls. However, it added that the Association had been 'extremely fortunate in the happy relationships ... between [it] and the Board of Trade' and paid tribute to the 'arduous work done by representatives of the Board'.[8]

Rather than the 'elderly office boys of Whitehall' it was more usually the staff of the industry associations themselves who had the job of producing the final versions of the paperwork – detailed specifications and others – on which the Utility scheme depended. A surviving example is the 46-page treatise on Maximum Selling Prices for Utility Apparel produced by the 'Utility Section' of the Wholesale Gowns, Mantles and Millinery Association (WGA) at the end of March 1942 (if they had not had access to a full price list before then, it was small wonder that many shopkeepers had found Utility a puzzle). The index runs to some 500 lines, covering the enabling legislation, descriptions of cloth, clothing prices, the use of cut, make and trim contractors, the use of other contractors, allowable costs and the mechanics of price fixing.

Even so, as a guide for manufacturers, wholesalers and retailers, the authors admitted that it was not exhaustive; to produce such a work would be pointless because, requiring so many months to compile, it would be out of date before getting into the hands of the trade. All this, thought the WGA, was nobody's fault: civil servants in the Board of Trade and in the Central Price Regulation Committee had been 'extremely courteous and helpful'. The whole thing was just too complex. The best that could be achieved was an indication to traders of the sort of calculations most likely to lead to a true selling price. Regrettably, despite the WGA's kind words about the helpfulness of officials, the Guide, which contained several worked examples of the 'Purchase Tax at one sixth of 50/- less 3 and three quarter percent discount' variety, appeared only weeks before Purchase Tax was removed from Utility garments.

Despite the ardours of form filling and the ostensibly low profit margins, the judgement of one leading commentator was that by the end of the war a good many, perhaps even most, manufacturers had grown to favour Utility: '... four factory men out of five in any industry, the world over, like certainty without worry. The fifth likes to experiment and keeps the others alive' said Wadsworth in his essay on the cotton industry and Utility.[9] If not enthusiastic, he thought that manufacturers were at least tolerant of the production of Utility cloth and garments which offered them real advantages: simplicity; a guaranteed, captive coupon-holding market, with raw materials, cash flow and profit all predictable – or as close to predictable as enemy action would permit.

However bureaucratic, lacking in innovation or excitement firms might have found making Utility cloth and garments, it was, after all, a good deal better than having the factory destroyed by bombing, closed as part of the concentration scheme or moved to another part of the country. As the physical threat of war receded, so impatience with Utility and the other clothing regulations grew stronger. The post-war period saw the manufacturers' and retailers' associations lobbying more vigorously for the ending of Utility, while the trades unions campaigned for its retention – just one symptom of the increasing polarization within British industry, as the wartime alliance between Government, capital and labour disintegrated.

NOTES

1   Settle, 1959, p47.

2 PRO, BT 64/182.
3 M-OA Topic collection 4/E and FR 1143; the series of reports was by 'P.N.', identified as Priscilla Novy, née Feare, who illustrated some with her own pencil sketches.
4 PRO, INF, 1/129.
5 M-OA, Topic Collection 4/E; Ann Seymour, described as wearing a simple black dress with a metal filigree brooch at the neck, also claimed that the *Sunday Chronicle* had lifted words and pictures from her own *Woman & Beauty* article.
6 Hargreaves and Gowing, 1951, p462.
7 *Journal of Society of Dyers & Colourists*, March 1944, p53; Sir Thomas had been speaking, on 28 Oct 1943, to members of the West Riding section of the Society.
8 Warwick MSS, 222.
9 Wadsworth, 1948, p96.

CHAPTER 4

'The bugbear of every mother':
Utility Boots and Shoes

'A pair of shoes for a child of three costs around 12/6 [63p]
and no pair ... lasts more than 3 weeks without repair.'
O. A. MacIver, 'Family Life in War Time', 1946

'The retailer has had great difficulty just after the
inception of wooden soled footwear in persuading ...
customers to buy this shoe.'
Boots Trades' Association Gazette, August 1944

Lord Woolton, in advising the Cabinet economic committee in March 1940 that any Utility scheme should include footwear, showed greater perception than those Ministers and officials who thought it was all about 'standard suits': however important a good suit might be to a working man, boots and shoes for the family always seemed likely to take priority.

As with wool and cotton, the Government in 1940–1941 had an urgent need to conserve rapidly diminishing stocks of hides and rubber from sources such as South America and Malaya. All available hides and leather were bought on behalf of the Government by the Leather Control and allocated to manufacturers. Rubber footwear, as we shall see, was less easily provided for. The shortage was made worse by the fact that shoes were likely to get harder wear in wartime conditions: a higher proportion of the population at work, plus restrictions on public and private transport, would mean more people walking further.

All this was no more than common sense, but Woolton also drew upon his previous experience in the footwear business: before the war, apart from his chairmanship of Lewis's, he had been a leading figure in the Boot Manufacturers' Federation; in 1939 Chamberlain sought his advice on how best the Ministry of Supply could equip the army with boots (in the First World War Woolton had also worked in the War Office contracts department). With him Woolton brought Major

Stratton, also from Lewis's; between them, Woolton claims, they were able to make sure that '... the whole [footwear] trade bent their energies to the task of ensuring that supplies were available. ... Army boots were always delivered up to time and caused me no trouble.'[1]

In the First World War proposals for a 'standard boot' had been put forward, in 1917–1918 but, as with the largely abortive 'standard clothing' scheme of that period, little came of them. During the inter-war period a number of changes in style and construction of footwear then took place, as recorded by the chronicler of the industry, June Swann.[2] Among male customers brown shoes started to outstrip black in popularity; in women's shoes the wedge heel, platform sole and a general increase in bulk, with shoes coming up to the ankle, were accompanied by a 'surge of colours' (although that last innovation became more prominent during the war when bright colour might conceal the use of poor quality materials). The average size of women's shoes in the 1930s had risen to $5\frac{1}{2}$, compared with the 2–3 of Edwardian times. There were a number of technical innovations. Moccasins for women were introduced and zips were increasingly used; in 1940 Churchill was able to sport black boots with zip fasteners to accompany his siren suit.

Significantly, by the late 1930s the British Footwear Manufacturers Federation (BFMF) was reporting a substantial increase in imports, particularly of cheap shoes from central Europe. Among British manufacturers the index of production, taking 1930 as 100, had reached only 107.9, and the BFMF estimated unemployment in the industry at around 11 per cent. Demand for shoes was relatively inelastic. The status of design in the industry was said to be low; although at the top end of the market a designer might be paid as much as £2,500 a year, most manufacturers relied on freelance 'designers' who merely copied European or US designs, often from magazine illustrations, at 10/- (50p) a time. Little or no thought was given to the health implications of shoe design; the Czech firm Bata was exceptional in setting up a design team for the UK market.[3]

Against this background of a relatively uninspired performance by UK manufacturers, in December 1939 Government and BFMF faced a steep rise in the price of imported hides. This in turn influenced the price of British hides and hence manufacturers' profit margins, retail prices of footwear having been brought under control, with others, early in the war. Informal discussions began between officials and the trade on some limitation of the total volume of production as well as a reduction in the number of styles. As with clothing and other sectors, footwear firms were subject from 1941 onwards to a policy of concentration, welcomed by many firms because it seemed to offer at least some continuity to a proportion of existing manufacturers. One final piece of background was that when Purchase Tax was introduced footwear, like clothing, was at first taxed, some at 33.3 per cent, most at 16.66 per cent. Rationing and 'austerity' style restrictions were put in place: a pair of men's boots took seven coupons, a pair of women's shoes five; a complete ban on rubber soles and heels followed in 1942.

Up to the early part of 1941 the BFMF had been talking mainly to the Ministry of Supply, which was responsible for Leather Control, but in June 1941 the Board of Trade appointed a Director of Civilian Footwear – H. G. Durston, a former president of the Leicester Footwear Manufacturers Association. Much of the detail concerning the difficulties of setting up the Utility footwear scheme comes from the voluminous correspondence between Durston, based in Leicester, and the Board of Trade's IM department on Millbank, in London. (When Durston retired in 1944 he was replaced by Major Stratton who combined control of civilian and forces footwear. At the same time the BoT scored an inter-departmental victory by wresting leather control from the Ministry of Supply; at that stage of the war planning for demobilization outfits, including shoes, was beginning to take higher priority than ensuring distribution of army boots.)

Following the precedent of the Utility clothing scheme, discussions about a 'national mark Utility footwear scheme' took place between July and October 1941, involving Durston in Leicester, IM department in London, the BFMF and other trade bodies. There was a good deal of resistance in the industry: 'it is not necessary for official regulation of a restrictive character to be imposed on the industry' claimed the BFMF,[4] which had already put forward its own 'schedules of restrictions' on design 'to prevent waste and ensure manufacture of durable footwear'. Individual firms did not believe that the Utility scheme would guarantee better supplies of leather, which was their overriding concern, and claimed that there would be a tendency to produce up to the maximum Utility price, so cutting out stocks of cheaper shoes.

Mr Clark, of C. & J. Clark, argued that Utility specifications would mean firms having to use more labour; though neither the BFMF nor the Board of Trade understood this argument. Not surprisingly, in real life the numbers employed in the industry continued to decline sharply from the 1939 level of 135,000, to 100,000 in 1942 after the introduction of Utility, and eventually to 95,300 in mid-1945.[5]

From October onwards Durston was sending almost daily minutes to Millbank, showing that he was not convinced that Utility was the best way to ensure the maximum quantity of boots and shoes for the civilian market. He claimed that would best be left to 'trade ingenuity, together with enforced and overriding economy arising from strict rationing [of raw materials]'.[6] Price control together with 'control of extravagant styling' (that is, 'austerity' rules similar to those for clothes) and 'rigid economy in usage of materials' were Durston's preferred tools; he visualized the job of allocating raw materials and of hearing appeals from aggrieved manufacturers being done by local production advisory committees, made up of industry representatives.

Durston's lack of enthusiasm was at least partly inspired by the feeling that Utility planning and control were in the hands of Ministers and officials in London; he would, not unnaturally, have preferred to see schemes run from Leicester. He was also anxious to gain personal control over the allocation of raw materials. Later in the war further arguments broke out between Leicester and the rest of the Board of Trade, when much of IM department moved to Bournemouth, occupying hotels on the west cliff; Durston immediately complained that it would be intolerable if all correspondence about footwear prices had to be routed via the south coast (in fact that aspect of the work stayed in London).

Although the tone of Durston's correspondence with Millbank was sometimes querulous, in his discussions with the trade associations he was happy to take credit for the Utility idea. IM officials in London countered Durston's objections by pointing out, first, that Utility was planned to apply to only 50 per cent of footwear production, leaving plenty of scope for the trade to exercise its 'ingenuity'. Secondly, although reliance on price control might allow more flexibility, with manufacturers able to use leather of different qualities according to availability, it would also tempt them to concentrate on those lines which offered the highest profit. In any case, by autumn 1941 a number of committees were already working on the Utility specifications; by February 1942, with Hugh Dalton installed as President of the Board of Trade, Ministerial support for Utility strengthened.

Before then, the first job tackled by Durston and other BoT officials was to estimate the total quantity of different kinds of leather available. The Ministry of Supply, put out by not having been involved in the Utility footwear exercise from the outset, commented that there was likely to be a 'bad fit' between the over-elaborate specifications being drawn up and the supplies of leather actually available. The manufacturers themselves continued to argue (according to BFMF minutes) that it would be impossible to predict how much of each different quality leather would be available. It would be better to leave it to market forces, allowing firms to make the largest total number of shoes they could, with customers left 'to maintain the standards of durability in accordance with the public's continuing demand for stouter footwear'.

These arguments were overridden. As with cloth and clothing, officials worked on the specifications with trade association representatives under the auspices of the BSI. Minimum standards were set for quality of materials; also the number of pieces (of leather) to be allowed in uppers and linings was specified, within limits that would 'ensure economical usage of material and labour without seriously detracting from appearance'.[7] There was a separate committee for each section of the industry: heavy boots, men's, women's, boys' and girls', infants' and high grade. Within each category the committees had to consider what they thought were the most essential types of footwear and how far stocks of raw material would permit their continued manufacture. Eventually it was agreed that within each type there should be four grades: cheap or lower medium; medium; best; high grade. On that basis a total of 116 individual specifications appeared in seven booklets published by the BSI, with new editions appearing at intervals.

Detailed schedules listed recognized types of shoe – for example *Mens Oxford, apron front* – which would qualify as Utility, but there was no absolute ban on other styles; any design of upper could be produced provided it covered the foot. There were pages of 'working particulars' for construction, materials, linings, fabric lining, bottoms, heels, closing, sock, laces, puff, shank, finishing and so on.[8]

Agreeing the different grades and specifications was at best only half of the problem; the job of fixing maximum prices for every grade within each category was 'almost one more for a soothsayer than for an accountant', wrote Durston in May 1942 – only a month before the scheme was due to come into operation. The difficulties arose from a combination of causes: differences in quality of materials; varying wage rates across the country; the fact that a firm's profit would depend, among other things, on how much of its capacity was being used. Firms calculated their production costs inconsistently; sometimes foremen were included in direct costs, sometimes in overheads. Some manufacturers, notably members of the Rossendale Valley Boot and Shoe Manufacturers Association (RVBSMA), tried to build in extra costs for having to employ 'green', that is untrained, labour in wartime. The BFMF argued that, because maximum prices would have to take account of the least efficient firm in the country, prices would tend to rise. Rather than applying Utility across the whole range of qualities, it would have been better to restrict it to the 'middle' 50 per cent – that is, between the upper and lower quartiles of the price range.

There were differences between the major, national trade associations on one side, and the RVBSMA on the other. The Rossendale firms felt that they had been left out of early discussions on the scheme, suspecting Durston of favouring the rival, largely Midlands, association. Rossendale firms were apparently not equipped to make shoes with the better quality 'bend' leather at the prices suggested for Utility; a special category had to be inserted into the schedules, allowing Rossendale factories to use shoulder leather to produce a shoe at a price higher than those made in the Midlands. Durston suspected that what the Rossendale firms really wanted was part of the allocation of scarce 'bend' leather. Ensuring consistent quality within each Utility grade was a constant problem; late in 1942 IM department in London received a number of complaints from customers who objected to finding the same number of coupons for an 'ordinary Rossendale Valley cheap shoe' as for the better quality Midlands product. Eventually the profit margin throughout the industry was fixed at 4.75 per cent on returns; Durston's 'soothsaying' accountants had suggested 3.5 per cent, while manufacturers had pressed for 5 per cent and continued to argue that a higher margin should apply to better quality shoes.

Further complications arose because large manufacturers like Barratt and Clark sold their products both through independent wholesalers and retailers and through shops which they owned themselves. As with clothes, manufacturers were constrained both by a fixed ceiling price and the 4.75 per cent profit margin; independent distributors were required to work only within the ceiling price, regardless of percentage profit. Special rules were introduced for 'composite businesses' which should have meant that manufacturers would transfer footwear from factory to their own warehouses at the same price as to outside distributors. Board of Trade officials believed that several major firms were 'doing very odd things', including counting distribution costs twice during the costing process.[9] Despite their suspicions (which were not finally resolved until 1946 when the trade associations reached an agreement on discounting), officials were reluctant to move against the large firms in the early days of the scheme. First, it was argued, all firms were faced with a severe shortage of raw materials and punitive action would simply depress morale. Secondly, as Durston had pointed out, calculating production costs was far from an exact science.

The legislative framework for the scheme, the *Utility Apparel (Maximum Prices and Charges) Order*, 1942, was published on 30 January 1942, to come into effect six months later, in June, a deadline which Dalton insisted must be met. 50 per cent of all footwear production – 75 per cent in the case of children's shoes – had to be of Utility specifications. The required Utility proportion rose to 70 per cent at the end of 1942; within the total, the proportion devoted to each quality had to be the same as the manufacturer had supplied to the retail trade in 1939. The trade associations, explaining the scheme to their members, used the 1939 price brackets as the simplest way of describing the Utility grades.

Apart from the Utility scheme, rationing and other restrictions, another preoccupation of the footwear section of IM Department was the consequences of the ban on the use of rubber for soles and heels, both on Utility and non-Utility footwear. This was a serious issue from the beginning of the war. Clerks in the footwear section spent much time dealing with complaints from farm workers and others to whom rubber boots were essential, but who were unable to find reliable supplies. Board of Trade Ministers rashly invited members of the public who had complaints about the quality of rubber boots to wrap

63

up the offending articles and send them to the Board of Trade so that the fault could be taken up with the manufacturers.

Many people did so, not always troubling to clean the boots too scrupulously first; the influx of untidy and odorous parcels was stored in a cupboard in IM's cramped offices, first in the former ICI headquarters on Millbank, later in the requisitioned Dolphin Square apartment block, half a mile upstream.[10] Shortage of leather and rubber also led the Board of Trade into discussions with the Clogmakers Association and others in the trade about the design, manufacture and marketing of wooden-soled shoes. Women's summer sandals, with canvas uppers and wood soles, had been imported from Europe during the 1930s.[11] At least one pair of Utility sandals, from 1943, with clog sole and plastic straps reinforced with leather to take the lace, survives (in Northampton museum: see Plate 5).

The dilemma which the Board of Trade faced in trying to increase sales of wooden soled footwear was that, although clogs had been practical and popular for traditional hard-wear occupations in mill or factory, the workers in those occupations were enjoying a boom in earnings and consequently wanting to move up-market in their choice of footwear. In the 1930s Mass Observation had found one manufacturer in 'Worktown' (Bolton) selling up to 1,000 pairs a week, but by 1940 that figure had fallen to 150–200.[12] Nationally, production of wooden soled shoes for women did reach substantial figures by the autumn of 1943, but the trade criticized the government for being too slow to remove Purchase Tax and to reduce the coupon value of clogs – a more likely way to tempt women to switch to wooden soles than any price differential.

In 1943 *Good Housekeeping* published helpful tips on how to look after wooden soled shoes, and how to walk in them:

'When you first put on a pair of these shoes, you'll feel at once how solid and comfortable they are – but you may have to adjust yourself by a little practice to the rolling tread of the rigid wooden sole. Experts tell us that the right way to do the "Wooden-Sole-Walk" is this. From the moment the heel touches the ground, the shoe should be allowed to "roll forward till the tip of the toe is reached".'

Readers were reminded that the wooden sole could not be repaired once it began to splinter. To offset these drawbacks it was claimed that '... the factory and mill workers of the North, who wear wooden-soled clogs, seldom suffer from colds and weak chests'.[13] IM Department officials persisted, persuading firms to experiment with hinged wooden soles – unsatisfactory because they let in the water. The BFMF opposed the whole idea; in 1944 it said that wooden-soled shoes, which lasted 'only a few days', were not even fit for free distribution to the desperate civilian population in newly liberated countries. The Board of Trade promoted a competition to find the best designed wooden soled shoe for women.[14] As well as clog soles, cork and raffia were used for women's sandals; French austerity sandals were said to have looked 'highly desirable'. Plastics were used during the war but blossomed later – synthetic soles in the 1950s, uppers in the 1960s.[15]

Apart from its uphill struggle to popularize clogs, the Board of Trade faced general criticism of Utility footwear from manufacturers, retailers and customers. A comparison of the number of times subjects occur in the index to the House of Commons Official Report (Hansard) shows 40 entries for footwear during a 12-month period, compared with no more than 50 for all other types of clothing, including uniforms. Most comment was adverse; in a debate on industrial concentration and the retail trade, however, not long after Utility goods began to appear in the shops, one MP (Mrs Adamson, Dartford, Labour) was 'pleased that the Board of Trade has eliminated the nasty, cheap shoddy shoe', making it possible for 'ordinary folk to get a good and pleasing design at a popular price', although she rather spoiled the effect by adding that there were not enough in the shops, nor had she actually bought any herself.[16]

By far the greatest number of complaints, and the most vociferous, were about children's shoes; it was said that children were being kept away from school because the quality of shoes was too poor (an alternative explanation was that unscrupulous parents were using up all the family's coupons). During a debate, in October 1944, on the Vote of Credit in Supply Committee, Hugh Dalton was in full flow on Utility products in general ('good and shapely, useful and durable products') when interrupted by an MP (D. L. Lipson, Cheltenham, Independent) complaining about children's shoes letting in the rain; Dalton had to admit that this was a 'sore subject'.[17]

In the summer of 1945 the periodical *Social Work*, published by the Family Welfare Association, distributed a questionnaire entitled 'The Effect of War Conditions on Domestic Life and Economy', the questions covering a number of aspects of family life, including food, household textiles, clothes and shoes. From that survey the journal concluded that it was impossible to keep a child adequately shod on its own clothing coupons, for which a 'grey market' existed, with coupons changing hands at 2/- (10p) each. 'Footwear is the bugbear of every mother', said the editors; even secondhand shoes had vanished from the market. Poor quality shoes plus 'shapeless Utility stockings' were destroying the nation's feet: 'The number of foot clinics ... working at high pressure tell their own story'.[18] The Ministry of Information's Home Intelligence reports, too, contained frequent references to children's shoes. In November 1942 a majority of all the MoI's sources referred to the poor quality of children's shoes and wellington boots (by comparison, as we have seen, clothing was never cited by more than a minority of sources).

How much this was a real problem, how much perception, is difficult to say. Although consumption of most kinds of clothing fell during the war, sales of children's shoes remained at the same level, even though there were fewer children than pre-war. Limited choice of style and the undisputed shortage of rubber boots and plimsolls (favoured by children then much as the ubiquitous trainer is today) were probably more to blame for the complaints than an overall shortage or any general decline in quality. Indeed, the view of experts is that Utility boots and shoes compare well with the materials and workmanship of later decades; while initially decried by the trade as inferior to pre-war, Utility became accepted as a reliable standard which could be trusted.[19]

As with clothing, there were constant amendments and additions to the specifications. In 1944–1945 the style restrictions were relaxed, for example to allow the use of fur trimming. In 1948, when Utility accounted for well over 90 per cent of all footwear production (shortages of raw materials and labour by that point meant that total production was down by over 10 per cent compared with 1940), there were further discussions with the trade and the scheme was greatly simplified. The original rule that Utility shoes should 'cover the foot' was rescinded so that sling-back and peep-toe styles could be included; the limit on the number of pieces to be used in uppers was also removed. There were now only three grades of shoe, related primarily to the price bracket, each with ceiling prices fixed by reference to manufacturers' basic costs. More detailed standards were kept for children's shoes and for safety or protective footwear; the latter had to meet the BSI standard (953), introduced in 1945, which certified compliance with a drop test.

All other Utility footwear, post-1948, was described as being manufactured consistent with 'Principles of Good Shoemaking'. Manufacturers had to take 'reasonable care' to ensure that their methods, raw materials and components were such that shoes would give reasonable wear and satisfaction if properly used for the purpose for which they had 'reasonably' been made. 'Expert opinion' from within the trade itself was to judge whether footwear had met the 'Principles' and was made in conformity with good practice relative to the particular type, method of construction and grade of shoe. Unlike clothing, the BoT had a handful of technical officers covering a sample of 800 designated factories to check standards of production.

Where a manufacturer was alleged to be producing shoes below a reasonable standard, the Board of Trade would refer the case to a panel of assessors drawn from the trade associations 'with a view to taking such action as may be necessary'. Apart from the threat of withdrawing the Utility mark or publicizing the fault, it is difficult to see what that action might be. All this – the BSI standard, tests of reasonableness and fitness for purpose, a complaints procedure – might be argued to fall within the mainstream of post-war consumer protection, but it was far from the original Utility concept of fixed specifications and guaranteed quality.

In 1944 the BFMF had said that it would support the continuance of Utility after the war, provided prices were increased. Manufacturers were keen to keep the benefit of Purchase Tax exemption, which guaranteed a market for Utility products, but with higher profit margins. In 1945–1946 the Labour government set up a footwear working party which noted, among other things, the poor status which footwear designers had enjoyed pre-war. It also found that before the war the industry's research association had put forward the idea of a certificated mark, which would guarantee quality of materials, components and manufacture: 'this scheme is surely deserving of support' commented the working party, recommending the idea of a 'Hallmark of quality'. Until that could be agreed, the cheapest grade Utility specification should be used 'as a means of describing the minimum quality for children's and men's shoes'.[20]

The manufacturers were not enthusiastic. The BFMF pointed out that the controls, including Utility, plus uncertainties about service orders, always tended to affect firms unevenly and unpredictably: in some output was running at 130 per cent of their 1940 level, in others at only 40 per cent. The main problem in those post-war years remained the continuing shortage and rising price of imported leather. Allocation of leather to the trade was still controlled; for its part; the Treasury was pressing for the subsidy on imported skins to be abandoned. All this made it more difficult than ever to predict the price structure and profit margins for footwear; 'The confusion extended into the Board of Trade' was the BFMF's comment, while the devaluation of 1947 increased the cost of imported hides, squeezing margins still further. At the same time the threat that the Cold War would erupt into fighting (as indeed it did, in Korea) actually led the Board of Trade to do more work on how to impose tighter controls over leather and footwear if the need arose; 'The outbreak of war within the next 4 years would find the world supply position much worse than in 1939 – though even then immediate institution of controls was necessary'.[21]

Despite the worsening supply position – or perhaps because of it – by 1951 the BFMF was once again petitioning for the Utility footwear scheme to be wound up. Harold Wilson, as President of the Board of Trade, replied somewhat oddly that 'Government policy' did not allow him to abolish the scheme, but the ceiling prices for manufacturer and wholesaler were removed, keeping only the single retail price ceiling 'as a long stop'. In fact politically it was growing increasingly difficult to maintain the Utility schemes. Not only was there increasing opposition from producers and customers at home (and a sense that voters might prefer a less austere regime), but the revival of international trade and its increasing impact on the UK economy meant that changes would have to be made. This strongly influenced discussions within government and, with the return of the Conservatives in 1951, swiftly brought about the end of Utility.

That decision, and the genesis of the 'D' scheme which replaced Utility in 1952, are more fully explored in the next chapter. As a footnote to the story of Utility footwear, however, it is worth recording that the boot and shoe manufacturers who had lobbied to such good effect against Utility found themselves scarcely better pleased with the 'D' scheme. Whereas under Utility less than 5 per cent of the industry's output attracted Purchase Tax, suddenly it was estimated that around 40 per cent would do so. Consumer spending in general was in any case sluggish; sales stagnated, stocks were high and imports again threatening. Far from reporting a mood of triumph in the industry now that Utility was dead, *The Times* (17 March 1952) concluded that 'An air of despondency hangs over the footwear towns'.

NOTES

1 Woolton, 1959, p155.
2 Swann, 1982, pp69–70.
3 BoT Working Party Report, *Boots & Shoes*, 1946.
4 BFMF, Annual Report, 1941.
5 Hargreaves and Gowing, 1951, p641.
6 PRO, BT, 64/856.
7 Ibid.
8 *Utility Footwear Specification*, Book 34, 1945 (Northampton Museum).
9 PRO, BT, 64/135.
10 Recalled by Ellen Bretton, former BoT clerical officer, 1992.
11 Swann, 1982, p69.
12 Harrison, 1961, p32; 'A stay-a-bed ... of the thirties might be woken anywhere in Worktown by the sound of metal-shod wooden clogs upon the cobbled street'. By 1960 Harrison found the same manufacturer was down to 60–70 pairs a week.
13 Braithwaite et al., 1987, p109.
14 Ellen Bretton, conversation, 1992; Ellen Bretton, then Smith, was allowed to keep the winning entry, by Brevitt, but discarded them in 1947 on leaving Britain to work overseas.
15 Swann, 1982, p76.
16 HofC, Vol. 382, Col. 232.
17 HofC, Vol. 403, Col. 2713–2714; in what passes for wit in Parliamentary circles Lipson responded, 'They are a *wet* subject'.
18 MacIver, 1946, p422.
19 Swann, unpublished letter to the author, 1992.

20   BoT Working Party report, 1946.
21   PRO, BT 64/739.

Plate 1   Utility mannequin show, 1942 (Hulton Deutsch Collection)

Plate 2 Hugh Dalton (Hulton Deutsch collection)

Plate 3 Harold Wilson and Stafford Cripps, in the Board of Trade canteen
(Hulton Deutsch collection)

Plate 4   Design for
civilian
battledress
(Hulton
Deutsch
collection)

Plate 5   Ladies' Utility sandals, late 1940s (Northampton Museum)

Plate 6 Wartime bride Marcell Lestrange choosing Utility dresses; the shop
assistant cuts coupons from the clothing book (Imperial War Museum)

Plate 7 'Make do and Mend': a sewing class at work in South London
(Imperial War Museum)

of 54-in. wool cloth sold at the same time as a large handkerchief make 4½ plus ½, which equals 5 coupons.

85. What has to be done with the Clothing Book or Card of someone who has died ? It should be returned to the local Registrar of Births and Deaths together with the current Food Ration Books when the death is notified.

86. What is the Utility clothing scheme ? The scheme is intended to ensure adequate supplies of durable good quality clothing at *reasonably low prices*. A considerable proportion of the raw material and labour available is used for the production of Utility cloths and clothing. All Utility cloths and clothing including shoes must bear the official mark.

87. What has been done to limit rises in the price of clothing ? For all Utility cloth and clothing maximum prices and maximum margins of profit have been fixed ; for non-Utility cloth and clothing there are no fixed maximum prices because qualities and types vary too much. But to avoid profiteering, the profit which any trader is permitted to make is controlled.

Local price regulation committees have been formed to see that these regulations are carried out.

Hotel Imperial, Inverness.

Amicable House, 252, Union Street, Aberdeen.

1, Culverden Gardens, Tunbridge Wells.

Oxford Street Chambers, Oxford Road, Reading.

Lombard House, Great Charles Street, Birmingham, 3.

Ministry of Commerce, Donegal Square East, Belfast.

Albion Chambers, Bristol, 1.

Northern Assurance Bldgs., Albert Square, Manchester, 2.

88. Are there any restrictions on style in making clothing ? Yes ; various restrictions in the making of garments have been introduced to save labour and material. They are to be found in the Making of Civilian Clothing (Restrictions) Orders.

89. Do these restrictions apply only to Utility clothing ? No ; they apply to garments of all types specified in the Orders whether or not they are made from Utility cloth.

90. If I provide my own cloth may I have a garment made up not complying with the restrictions ? No ; anyone carrying on the business of making up clothing must comply with the restrictions whether the material is supplied by the customer or by the person making the garment.

91. Are there any special arrangements for disabled persons ? Yes ; tailors are permitted to make wider trousers for persons wearing calliper splints or artificial legs.

92. If I make up my clothes at home, need they comply with the restrictions ? No ; the restrictions do not apply to the garments you make for yourself.

Plate 8   A page from the 1942–1943 Clothing Quiz booklet, showing the official Utility mark.

Plate 9   Utility fashions illustrated in *Weldon's Ladies Journal*, January, 1942 (Bath Museums Service)

CHAPTER 5

Post-War and New Look

'Wars end tidily in the history books, with the moment of signing a document, but there was no single finishing line for the shortages of food, clothes and fuel and all the aspects of austerity which gave a dull grey tinge to post-war life.'

Susan Cooper, in *Age of Austerity*, 1963

'There can be no question of the entire unsuitability of these new fashions for our present life and times.'
Picture Post, on the New Look, 1947

Utility was not a single once-for-all set of rules; the schemes emerged piecemeal and were continually modified up to 1951, less than a year before the Orders governing them were annulled: it had become known as the 'Utility patchwork'. We have seen how the original 'three figure' cloth specifications for cotton and rayon were tightened up; new specifications were added during the war. From 1944–1945 onwards there was a further succession of changes to all parts of the clothing controls.

From 1944 the Board of Trade clothing 'budget', the civil servants' calculation of total cloth production, was no longer divided into the separate cloth specifications; two years later the system of cloth certificates and the allocation of cloth to individual manufacturers were also abandoned. By the end of the war, therefore, much of the central planning of cloth production had effectively ceased. Essential elements of Utility – control of price and of quality – remained. Utility clothes (except those made from fur and fully fashioned stockings) and shoes benefited not only from Purchase Tax exemption, but from a subsidy on cloth, introduced in 1944. In the year 1945–1946 that subsidy cost the taxpayer £4 million, about the same as the subsidy on cheese and a small fraction of the £189 million spent on food subsidies as a whole. As Britain's economic and financial position deteriorated in 1947 and 1948, however, the subsidies were withdrawn.

Throughout 1944 and the first half of 1945 stocks of clothes at wholesalers fell. The civilian clothing ration had to be reduced from 48 coupons per 12 months, first to just over 41 and then, in September 1945, to 36; the impact was softened by the fact that some garments were 'down pointed' – fewer coupons had to be given up per garment. The shortfall in clothing stocks was not made up until the second half of 1946.[1]

Underlying all this was the devastation of the UK economy: overseas investment virtually gone, the loss of 50 per cent of the merchant fleet, run-down transport and manufacturing infrastructure, exports running at only 33 per cent of pre-war levels, and new debts of around £3 billion. Government posters exhorted ever greater efforts from the working population ('We Work or Want'). The first Christmas of peace promised to be a pretty dim one. The historian Peter Hennessy pictures the streets of London full of 'pale faces, drab often threadbare clothing with a sameness about it that came from rationing and standard (sic) Board of Trade apparel designs. Men all seemed to be wearing the same suit of the classic demob type.'[2]

So it seems surprising to find that the Board of Trade had decided, in mid-1944, to lift the style restrictions on men's outerwear. Hugh Dalton put a paper to the Lord President's Committee on 14 January that year, proposing that the trade should be allowed to start making non-austerity suits, primarily for demobilized servicemen. He did not want to give the public the impression that there was no longer any need for economy or for concentration on the war effort; he therefore proposed to down-coupon austerity suits (left in stock after the relaxation took effect) and up-coupon non-austerity suits. Dalton, who had so cheerfully defended the ban on trouser turn-ups two years earlier, was equally eloquent about its abolition, along with other restrictions:

'... we have done something to lift the morale of the men. The morale of the women has always been high, but that of the men has been depressed by not having enough pockets'.[3]

As we have seen, children's clothes, rather than men's suits, had been the real cause of worry and complaint. On the other hand the people who took decisions – Ministers and senior civil servants – and those who wrote the leading articles which they read, were mainly men, and men to whom suits were important. Ministers believed that they had to avoid discontent among demobbed troops by offering them a superior style of suit; having agreed that, it would have been difficult to continue with 'austerity' suits for everyone else. A year later a general range of higher quality Utility clothing was announced, due to reach shops in spring 1946; men's ready-to-wear suits in the new range would cost up to £8.12.5 (£8.63) compared with £5.6.11 (£5.35) in the older range. Following these changes, the 1946 *Clothing Quiz* boasted both that 75 per cent of garments sold were Utility, and that the new higher quality ranges were meeting the needs of customers who were prepared to pay higher prices. Around this time designs in women's outerwear also changed: hard corners softened, waists were more pronounced, coats more gracefully flared.[4]

During the first half of 1945 the Board of Trade was talking to the Treasury and to industry associations about the overall future of clothing control. Dalton, whose main preoccupation was still with the cost of living, promised that all style restrictions should end when circumstances permitted, but price control must remain. The Wholesale Clothing Manufacturers Federation advised that, while materials and labour remained so short, it would be pointless to remove restrictions; no changes should be made unless ceiling prices could be held. The Federation also recommended that minimum making specifications should be kept after the war, to stop shoddy workmanship. The Government was anxious to grant further rewards, even those as trivial as allowing extra trimmings on women's underwear, trying to persuade the trade that this could be achieved within unchanged ceiling prices; 'I am not sure if we can hold this position' wrote a dubious official.[5] In October 1945, it was agreed that style restrictions on women's outerwear, underwear and children's wear could be lifted the following March, to coincide with the normal seasonal changes in production and stock release.

So far as Utility was concerned, more and more variants were inserted into the specifications and price schedules; by 1951 there were over 1,000 different specifications for non-wool cloths. Even so, Board of Trade officials were constantly pressed to give individual manufacturers special permission to apply the Utility mark to goods which were not listed in the general Orders: industrial clothing, such as fishermen's jumpers, was one example, but there were others among ordinary civilian clothing. Many hundreds of such special licences were granted.

The discarding of specifications for the making of Utility footwear in 1948 (except for children's shoes and protective footwear) which we have already noted (Chapter 4) was, in 1950, extended to hosiery and knitwear; broad general descriptions started to appear, such as 'Vest, athletic, not less than 30% wool with other fibre'. Finally, in 1951, so-called 'flexible specifications' were introduced across the whole range of cotton and rayon cloths, allowing a great variety of construction under the Utility label. These loose descriptions remained alongside the 1,000 or so detailed specifications until the scheme was wound up in 1952.

Probably the most emotive issue in the post-war clothing market was that of fully-fashioned nylon stockings. Next to children's wear, stockings were the major preoccupation of housewives throughout the war. Nylon stockings had first been sold (in Wilmington, Delaware) in the 1930s, with the promise that they would halve stocking bills without loss of glamour. By the end of the war, UK nylon production was about one million pounds (weight) per year, but none of it for civilian consumption; the Board of Trade issued a special *Nylon News* leaflet in which the helpful 'Mrs Sew and Sew' gave some advice on how to treat second-hand parachute nylon.

In 1945 manufacturers were keen to develop this market and, correctly or not, women believed there had been a promise of nylons for all, a promise which could certainly not be fulfilled. At the end of the year industry sources told civil servants that they were aiming at 18 million pairs a year, when the total market was estimated at 130 million pairs; even that was only a guess, since British Nylon Spinners were unable to say how much yarn they could produce, nor what it would cost. A year later a Pathé news item attacked the failure of the manufacturers to 'meet their pledge of nylons for every woman who wanted them', adding parenthetically that 'the Board of Trade said nothing'.

Aside from technical and other problems of the manufacturers, a good reason for reticence was that officials were locked in discussions about how to treat this new product for Purchase Tax purposes. As we have seen, there had always been skirmishes between Board of Trade and Treasury officials, the latter suspecting the former of wanting to expand the range of Utility, tax-free goods almost to infinity. During 1945 the two Departments discussed the tax position, first, of silk-embroidered underwear (Treasury eventually agreeing that Purchase Tax would be waived), then of nylon stockings. Here Treasury officials were less easily persuaded. They could see that there was a tremendous pent-up demand for this product: 'a proper source from which considerable revenue would be derived'. Agreement was reached fairly quickly that 'art silk' (rayon) stockings should continue to be tax exempt. There was then a suggestion that, for silk and nylon stockings, a subsidiary Utility mark might be introduced which would carry the quality guarantee but not the tax exemption.[6] BoT officials became champions for the women of Britain:

'the inclusion of nylon stockings in the range will enhance the prestige of the Utility mark ... the long-promised nylon wear represents to the women of today what hats represented to the women of yesterday ... to impose Purchase Tax on Utility nylon stockings is psychologically bad.'[7]

HM Customs & Excise (collectors of Purchase Tax) seemed surprisingly relaxed: the loss of revenue would be no more than £1 million a year and it would be anomalous to apply the tax to nylon and not to rayon. Probably the crucial argument, however, was the pragmatic one: there was no hope of the industry being able to produce enough nylons to meet the demand at tax-free prices; however small the revenue, the imposition of the tax would help to bring down demand to somewhere near the level which manufacturers could satisfy. Eventually, therefore, it was agreed that fully-fashioned stockings, of whatever material, should carry Purchase Tax at 33.3 per cent; the October 1946 revision to Utility specifications for knitted goods and hosiery included five for fully-fashioned stockings, of which two were nylon; maximum retail prices per pair were 8/3 – 9/10 (42–48p).

In the case both of nylon and silk stockings (which Board of Trade hopefully but unsuccessfully suggested might be included in the Utility range, in 1946), the Treasury relied on a number of arguments relating not only to potential loss of revenue but, significantly, to the fact that if foreign imports of stockings were taxed and British ones not, the UK would be seen to be in breach of the International Trade Charter. This question of import discrimination would become the central issue in discussions about the future of Utility clothing. Before exploring those arguments, however, it is worth pausing to look at the change in the design of women's clothing which swept across Britain in 1947.

After the fall of France, in 1940, the Paris fashion industry, under the leadership of the *Chambre Syndicale*, managed to fight off the threat of closure or wholesale removal to Germany or Austria. Paris wartime fashions, produced largely for the benefit of German officers' wives, were judged to be 'vulgar, ill-proportioned ... supremely un-chic'.[8] Un-chic or not, the industry emerged from the war relatively intact and determined to regain its world role, so that by 1947 there was a 'real re-discovery of Paris flair and inventiveness'. In February Christian Dior's collection (*Life* magazine is generally credited with christening it the 'New Look') was judged to have demolished at a stroke the wartime line, epitomized by Utility, of square shoulders, the narrow short skirt and flat-hipped jacket. Instead, the fashion writers reported

> 'Shapely skirts, flowing to mid-calf with ... a myriad of hand-pressed pleats [which] brought sculpture back into fashion, moulding drapery round the figure and highlighting the body's natural curves'.

It was, writes Jane Dorner[9] like 'a breath of fresh air', as Dior dramatically dropped hemlines, using lavish amounts of fabric and inventing new ways of cutting and constructing dresses – for example the introduction of paper-stiff nylon linings (the fact that he was backed by the Boussac textile empire was not irrelevant). Janey Ironside, later Professor of Fashion Design at the Royal College of Art, recalled it as being 'like a new love affair ... a new look at life. Women had the chance to transform themselves from Cinders to Cinderella.'[10] Other writers sensed echoes of the elegance of previous centuries.

While fashion journals applauded Dior's boldness, Parisians were apparently horrified; '40,000 francs for a dress, and our children have no milk', women were said to have screamed; in one heavily reported incident, a Dior dress was torn off the back of a model in the rue Lepic. When Dior went to the US on a promotional tour, he was met by 'Christian Dior Go Home' placards. We may suspect that much of this outrage was neither spontaneous or disinterested, and perhaps that Dior himself was not too distressed by the publicity.

Well before Dior arrived, manufacturers in the US had viewed with distaste the efforts of Paris to re-colonize the American market. Even in 1944 it had been pointed out that there was some irony in the French government helping the *Chambre Syndicale* to sell dresses overseas, while simultaneously appealing to Americans to donate clothes to the newly liberated people of France. The irony was all the sharper because the US government's own L85 making-up restrictions remained in force.

In Britain Stafford Cripps and Harold Wilson, successively Presidents of the Board of Trade in 1947, denounced the waste of materials and labour on these 'imbecilities'. From the back benches Mrs Mabel Ridealgh (Ilford, Labour) weighed in:

> 'Can anyone imagine the average housewife and businesswoman dressed in bustles and long skirts ... running for buses and crowding into tubes and trains? The idea is ludicrous. The New Look is too reminiscent of a caged bird's attitude. I hope our fashion dictators will realise the new outlook of women and give the death blow to any attempt at curtailing women's freedom.'[11]

But against the tide of fashion these were Canute-like gestures. The popular press might editorialize against these 'Fashions for Yesterday' but it still gave them first-class pictorial coverage, with even the *Daily Herald* illustrating the Dior dresses. Much was made of the fact that many of the dresses demanded the wearing of whale-bone corsets 'like the one Grandma wore'. *Picture Post* (27 September 1947) took up Mrs Ridealgh's 'dictators' tag, accusing the fashion designers of conspiring against women's freedom:

> 'Dior alters *your* shape to fit *his* clothes ... even if the many thousands of yards of material were available and every woman had enough coupons for an entire new wardrobe (the changes are so drastic that no compromise between old and new is possible) can anyone seriously contemplate hopping on a bus in a hobble skirt? Our mothers freed us from these in their struggle for emancipation ... in our own active workaday lives there can be no possible place for them' [emphasis added].

The British designer Cecil Beaton called the arrival of the New Look 'one of those rare moments ... when women staged an *abortive* revolt against the tyranny of a vastly expensive change that required the complete discarding of their old wardrobes'.[12] Painful struggles with money and coupons ensued; in 1947 Mrs June McDonald was secretary to the Housewives League; 40 years later she remembered having been very cross:

'... there was Christian Dior, lowering the hemlines almost to the ankle, with enormously full skirts and little slim tops ... nothing we had in the cupboard was any longer in fashion ... an awful lot of us said "Oh we can't afford it" ... but of course we did.'[13]

Mass Observation carried out two attitude surveys on the New Look. In 1947 they found that seven out of ten people (both sexes) were hostile. Twelve months later there was still opposition, but mainly from men over 35 who, MO judged, represented a shrinking minority:

'Differences between 1947 and 1948 are considerable. In 12 months two thirds of both men and women under 35 have revised their opinions ... by 1948 New Look has a majority of two to one in favour among *all* women and also among younger men (who, it seems, conform very much to feminine pattern in matters of fashion) [and] there are signs of acclimatisation even among the comparatively stable group of older men'[14]

The views of young men in those politically non-correct days were predictable:

'It is bringing into my vision a bevy of rather attractive females [who] bring some eagerly awaited glamour to an otherwise depressing world. ... It is pleasant walking through the town to college to see all the young women discarding their squarish fashions and wearing garments that let one see they have a curve here and there.'

Reaction within the industry revealed the usual divide between large and small firms. In spring 1947 a deputation of small clothing manufacturers called on the Board of Trade to impose a ban on longer skirts. Officials declined, pointing out that even during the war the Government had not attempted to impose an absolute or all-embracing ban on every fashion; Utility and austerity restrictions alike had left a good deal to the discretion of the individual maker-up. Despite Ministers' disapproving noises, they were not going to bring in such a ban now. Large firms, meanwhile, were gearing up as quickly as possible to copy and market the new styles. Dereta produced a New Look grey flannel suit, 700 of which were sold within a fortnight at one London store.

In the process Dior's line was 'modified for Liverpool Street in the rush hour', resulting in what Hopkins, historian of the New Look, terms the 'new-old look of bottleneck shoulders and rounded hips'. With the Board of Trade having decided not to legislate against the new skirt lengths, manufacturers found that they could use Utility cloth to produce acceptable styles within the broad church of this 'new-old look'. Cecil Beaton was thus right to say that the revolt against the New Look was, in the end, abortive. Dior and his competitors saw the New Look accepted, but egalitarianism also prevailed in the sense that it always does, with the most eye-catching extravagance of *haute couture*, the one-off garment designed and custom built for the cat-walk, adapted to fit, firstly, the templates and machines of the large-scale manufacturer and, secondly, the sizes and purses of millions of buyers.

It is therefore simplistic to think in terms of a battle between Utility and the New Look which the latter somehow 'won'. Given time, the industry was well able to produce designs using Utility fabrics and based on the skirt lengths and curves that had so startled Paris in February 1947. Although it is true that from 1947 onward a higher proportion of women's clothing was non Utility, even so Utility still accounted for over 80 per cent of all cotton and rayon cloth produced in Britain, cloth that could be made up only into Utility, price-controlled garments.

More profoundly, the New Look's advance across Britain symbolized the increasing importance of international trade in textiles and clothing. The import of Dior and other high fashion dresses was an example, if a minor one, of what was becoming a major dilemma for the British Government: on the one hand it wanted to nurture British manufacturers and protect British employment; on the other to stand by its international commitment to free trade – from which, as the Federation of British Industry (FBI) pointed out, Britain would be a major beneficiary. The ISLFD, which had helped create Utility in

1941, and other allies of the Board of Trade, such as the Model House Group of ready-to-wear manufacturers, were heavily involved in promoting exports of British fashions, especially to North America. This would be at risk if Britain were seen to renege on trade agreements.

The Board of Trade looked at ways of harnessing Utility to exports: 'good dollar exporters' (firms successful in selling to North America) might earn licences to sell on the home market as Utility, free of tax, any goods which they failed to sell in the dollar markets; a special higher-priced Utility range would have to be introduced to cope with this. The Utility scheme for fur garments was uniquely used to encourage exports by allowing manufacturers to sell fur coats on the home market in proportion to their export sales, taxed at 33.3 per cent rather than the 100 per cent which applied to such garments in general. Reluctantly, however, it was decided that extending such 'open favouritism' in the fiscal field across the whole range of Utility products would raise too many issues

To the economic pressure (constant exhortations to 'Export or Die' and the withdrawal of subsidies in 1947–1948) was added increasing political edge as the date for a general election drew closer. Up to 1947 Government controls had drawn comparatively little political fire; the Conservative *Industrial Charter*, published in May that year, endorsed the need for temporary controls and rationing (while attacking trade union restrictive practices). The impact of devaluation, the shortage of dollars and events such as the fuel shortage in the hard winter of 1947–1948, however, were combining to erode the Government's popularity. By 1950, the Conservative manifesto would feature a promise that controls would be cut to the minimum. In a preemptive move in the autumn of 1948, Harold Wilson promised a 'bonfire of controls'. In 1949 rationing of clothes (and sweets) was abolished, as was the Wool Control; in November Wilson repeated that

'... we want to get rid as quickly as possible of those controls which restrict the handling or sale or manufacture of goods to specified firms ... limiting competition and preventing the entry of ... enterprising, progressive and efficient firms.'[15]

The Government was trying to steer a middle course between

conflicting political aims: being seen to scrap controls could be popular with some voters, but everyone wanted prices to be kept down. In pursuit of the latter aim, in July 1949, Harold Wilson announced an average 5 per cent reduction in the maximum prices of Utility clothes, footwear and household textiles, a move bitterly attacked by retailers who would have to find the greater part of this saving. Facing down reaction from the Opposition benches, Wilson admitted that '... these changes will involve a good deal of additional work for the traders' and asserted (no evidence was produced) that retailers and wholesalers would largely be able to make up the savings by reducing staff: 'I think it is generally agreed ... that the staffs in the distributing trades have grown rather more than the nation can afford'.[16] The proportion of all clothes accounted for by Utility, he claimed, was increasing and he had every reason to suppose that it would continue to do so. With the election now less than a year away, the risk of infuriating the distributive trade was judged acceptable in order to continue to offer the electorate low fixed prices and the ostensible quality guarantee of Utility. By contrast the French government, which brought in a few small-scale quasi-Utility schemes in 1946–1947, deliberately favoured small shopkeepers by restricting 75 per cent of the sale of *produits d'utilité sociale* to the independent (*individuel*) retailers.[17]

Meanwhile, manufacturers were arguing that a significant part of UK exports consisted of higher-quality goods; if these exports were to be increased, makers needed greater freedom to experiment and introduce new designs at home. They were prevented from doing so because the home market was restricted by the incidence of Purchase Tax on non-Utility goods. Further, it was said, restricting the sale of higher quality and higher priced goods meant that the demand for craftsmen and skilled workers was reduced and recruitment discouraged, with possible long-term damage to industry. Finally, the clothing manufacturers said that the normal pattern was for new designs and styles to be introduced at the top end of the market first, then modified and copied by the large producers for the mass market. Stifling the so-called luxury trades at home must eventually have a bad effect on exports and on the capacity of UK industry as a whole.

However specious some of these arguments may have been, dividing the UK home market into tax-free (Utility) and taxable (non-Utility) was becoming an impossible position for the Government to maintain. Britain's trading partners stepped up their campaign against the unfair advantage which Utility gave British manufacturers. It had already been agreed in principle that importers could be licensed to put the Utility mark on furniture made outside Britain, provided it matched Utility quality and price ranges. In 1948–1949 a working party of civil servants looked at the possibility of extending this system to clothing and footwear. Reporting in April 1949, however, the working party decided that although the current arrangements for furniture should continue, it would be impossible to offer the same benefit to other imported goods without destroying the whole Utility structure.

By 1949–1950 it was clear that an overall review of Utility and Purchase Tax was inevitable. The Government, officials pointed out, could not go on forever basing Utility specifications and price control on wartime legislation – Regulations 55 and 55AB under the *Defence of the Realm Act*. New legislation was needed which might also tackle the thorny problem of imported 'Utility equivalent' goods. The Board of Trade line had moved closer to that of the Treasury; indirect taxation of manufactured goods was seen as an 'unfortunate necessity, which is to be preferred to financial instability or to a further increase in direct taxes ... a further extension of ... Utility in textiles would be a retrograde step'.[18] As the 1950 general election approached some hedging of bets can be detected among Board of Trade officials, while those in the Treasury remained antipathetic to Utility; its guarantee of quality and price stability could not compensate for the corresponding loss of revenue.

Customs and Excise was irritated by the scheme's administrative headaches, especially since control was in the hands of another Department; there was some suggestion that Customs & Excise should take powers to regulate a 'Customs mark' which would differentiate between taxable and non-taxable goods, cutting the ground from under the Utility mark. C & E officers collected examples of dishonesty in industry: some cloth manufacturers were entrusting the application of the Utility mark to sub-contractors (including a maker-up in Eire, which particularly riled the Treasury), then selling the cloth to members of the public who could have it made up into suits at higher-than-Utility prices, but free of tax.

After the 1950 general election Utility was at first discussed within the context of a proposed Economic Powers Bill. Harold Wilson argued for a separate Consumer Protection Bill, asking officials to think about a range of measures, including 'additional powers to safeguard the Utility programme', but also amendments to the Merchandise Marks Act (for example requiring the manufacturer's name to appear on all furniture, Utility and non-Utility) and setting up a network of consumer advice centres. The Labour government's slender majority, however, made immediate legislation impractical. In the meantime the CoI was asked to carry out a survey of public attitudes to Utility and to 'obtain some indication of public opinion in general on the subject of Government control'.[19]

The survey took a national sample of 2,594 adults; 75 per cent of them were found to understand that the Government controlled prices and issued specifications of Utility goods (87 per cent knew about Utility furniture and 28 per cent thought that there was a Utility crockery scheme), although only 47 per cent knew that Utility goods were free of Purchase Tax; 93 per cent remembered seeing the Utility mark. Other findings included:

- in answer to the question 'What is meant by Utility?', 26 per cent instanced quality control, 31 per cent price control;
- 26 per cent thought that Utility stood for 'good', 14 per cent for 'poor' quality;
- 60% favoured a permanent Utility scheme; 57% wanted it extended to other household goods;
- 83 per cent favoured Government price control; 49 per cent would do so even if it resulted in a narrower choice of goods;
- 57 per cent thought that something should be done to guarantee the quality of goods, especially clothing; 22 per cent thought manufacturers should be responsible for this, 13 per cent the Government;
- 49 per cent favoured some 'standardisation of styles' if that meant lower prices. 44 per cent thought that quality control would not affect prices but 31 per cent thought prices would go up;
- only 44 per cent said they looked for or asked for Utility by name, but between 70 per cent and 90 per cent had bought Utility goods of some kind, the highest proportion among buyers of children's clothing.

Compared with a similar survey in July 1948, the proportion in favour of having more Utility clothes in the shops was exactly the same (50 per cent) but the proportion in favour of extending Utility to other goods such as holloware had gone up from 53 to 57 per cent. Board of Trade officials reacted cautiously:

> 'The results of an attitude survey of this kind should be treated with greater caution than those of consumer surveys of a more factual kind. There is no doubt that what people want is high quality goods at low prices but there is not much evidence that they attach a lot of importance to how they get them. Insofar as the Utility schemes are favourably regarded the reason is not that people understand how they work ... they fail to realise the extent to which the restrictions on production have been relaxed, and still loosely associate Utility with good quality and/or controlled prices.'[20]

The survey did, however, provide helpful ammunition for Utility's political enthusiasts. The Government's natural supporters, the trades unions, had always advocated continuing and extending the Utility schemes. Less than a month after the defeat of Japan, a TUC resolution called for Utility and price control to be kept in order to foster good design and make sure that consumers got good value for money:

> '... the bounties of men coming home from the forces, and the savings of the workers, are going to be taken away from them in the purchasing of shoddy goods and profiteering ... if the present controls are removed.'[21]

Similar resolutions appeared each year; trades unions in the furniture industry insisted that the standard of the cheaper ranges of furniture had been raised 'by at least 50%' by the imposition of Utility specifications. In August 1951 the National Union of Tailors and Garment Workers were still calling for the reintroduction of subsidies on Utility clothing and the abolition of Purchase Tax on all clothing, both Utility and non-Utility, in order to keep down prices and preserve full employment. However lukewarm his officials may have been, and while continuing to seek maximum credit for abolishing controls, Harold Wilson regularly sang the praises of Utility. The Budget debate in April 1950 gave him an opportunity to accentuate the scheme's virtues and to snipe at the private sector:

'It was the intention of the Government that the Utility scheme, one of our greatest national assets – and a safeguard to the housewife in guaranteeing both quality and fair prices – should be maintained. The benefits of the scheme ... should be carried forward as a permanent feature of our economy. ... It was a matter of concern that Utility production in cotton ... had fallen so far short of our needs. There was evidence that spinners and weavers and highly organised finishing trades had been increasing their prices ... far more than was justified by the rise in the price of raw cotton; ... housewives would insist that further steps should be taken, not excluding the reimposition of ... controls.'[22]

A Labour election broadcast in the 1951 campaign promised that:

'We are going to develop the Utility clothing schemes. We have got so accustomed to reasonably priced Utility clothes ... that we sometimes forget what a boon they are ... the envy of countries where Tory policies are being followed. Our British Utility dresses are beating all competitors on the Paris market.'[23]

At the beginning of that year the Utility cloth range had again been extended by the inclusion of some better quality and more expensive woollen, worsted and worsted/rayon cloths, for making up into girls' outerwear. The summer 1951 issue of the Treasury's *Report to Women* concluded that:

'Utility schemes provide some guarantee of quality for money. It would appear therefore that if they continue to be backed by pressure of public demand, Utility schemes are likely to remain with us in one form or another for some time to come.'[24]

For 'pressure of public demand' one can read 'political will'. Despite bullish noises from the politicians, correspondence within Government and arguments from outside made it increasingly clear that survival of Utility in anything like its present form was unlikely. Manufacturers continued to emphasize the practical difficulties and anomalies of the schemes. The Overall Manufacturers Association (OMA), for example, giving evidence to the Board of Trade on cotton and rayon cloth, saw some advantages in Utility: cloth specifications enabled manufacturers to order with confidence in terms of quality and they hoped that this feature 'may be retained'. But the price control system on cloth had worked badly; there were long bureaucratic delays in fixing prices. Exemption from Purchase Tax was seen as important but illogical: some non-Utility boiler suits could now be produced, attracting tax, while Utility beach-wear did not; all leather footwear was tax-free, but rubber boots attracted tax. There was a general lack of flexibility; the Board of Trade issued special licences for non-standard lines, but what manufacturers wanted was a general extension of styles.[25] When the new 'flexible specifications' were introduced in 1951 the older, rigid ones were left in place, adding to the complexity of the rules and to the paperwork for manufacturers. The most serious defect of Utility on the home market was said to be the virtual absence of goods at prices immediately above the Utility range – the so-called 'blind spot' argument.

As always there was an element of wanting to have it both ways among manufacturers: they liked the certainty which long runs of standard products provided, but they also wanted the freedom to innovate and earn profits from new lines. In the longer term, as is argued in the next chapter, Utility's true legacy probably lay in the industry's acceptance of minimum manufacturing standards; at this stage, for example, the OMA got into discussions with the BSI about permanent standards of 'wearability' for overalls.

Being seen as a system which discriminated against imports, the risk of retaliation by Britain's trading partners remained a real threat. The GATT meeting which took place at Torquay in December 1950 intensified pressure on the British Government from other countries, notably Canada and the Netherlands, with the UK having to agree that discrimination by way of Purchase Tax exemption on Utility goods would be removed. By the following spring the new President of the Board of Trade, Hartley Shawcross, was adamant that a solution had to be found before the GATT met again in Geneva in September 1951: 'We have been in default so long that pleas of extenuating circumstances will command no sympathy'.[26]

Three possible solutions were put forward: allow imported goods to carry the Utility mark and thus escape tax; levy a lower rate of tax, say 10 per cent, on all textiles and footwear (both Utility and non-Utility, British and imported); or levy Purchase Tax on a sliding scale to get rid of the 'blind spot'. Shawcross inclined to the first of these; Britain's trading partners could be told in September that a new 'marking' scheme would be initiated and legislation introduced during the autumn. However, earlier discussion had already effectively discarded the idea. Further, the essential quality element of Utility would become hopelessly diluted; the Social Survey may have shown that only a minority of voters understood the relationship between Utility and quality, but the Government's supporters, including the trades unions, would be on the look out for any diminution of the value for money principle. Because of that sensitivity, and the Government's wafer-thin majority, Utility was not mentioned during the Budget debate of April 1951.

Before he left the Board of Trade, Harold Wilson had been one of those who opposed bringing imports into the scope of Utility, saying that GATT members should be satisfied with the setting up of a committee on Utility and Purchase Tax. He argued that the end of the link between Utility and tax exemption would make manufacturers less keen to concentrate on lower priced, good quality products. Hugh Gaitskell, as Chancellor of the Exchequer, and Douglas Jay, as Financial Secretary, persuaded Shawcross (at a meeting on 4 June 1951) that the committee should be announced during the summer, and Shawcross should tell the Canadians and Dutch that discrimination would be eliminated by the spring of 1952, but without hinting what the precise solution would be and without exposing the Government's Parliamentary difficulties.[27]

A former civil servant, Sir William Douglas, was appointed as chairman of the committee. Members were drawn from chambers of commerce, trades unions, manufacturers and retailers, and the press (G. D. N. Worswick, editor of the *Economist*). The token woman was Margaret Allen, a member of the Central Price Control Committee (Hugh Gaitskell turned down officials' recommendation of 'superior women' such as Lady Reading). Summarized, the terms of reference were:

'To review the present system of Purchase Tax affecting those classes of goods within which Utility schemes operate in relation to international agreements on taxation of imported goods, and to the interests of the export trade, manufacturers and consumers; to consider adjustments to the system and to submit recommendations, bearing in mind the need to maintain the advantages of Utility to consumers and the yield of Purchase Tax revenue.'

In fact the Ministerial and official discussions had already virtually agreed the solution. Following the meeting of a Cabinet Committee (GEN 358/1) on 16 March 1951, officials had been asked to devise a final refinement of Utility; their work resulted in what came to be known as the 'D' scheme. The essence of this was that no Utility goods should automatically be exempt from Purchase Tax. Within each range of goods for which Utility schemes existed, a fixed deduction would be made from the wholesale value averaged across Utility and non-Utility goods, and tax would be levied only on the difference between that 'D' value and the retail price. Imported and home produced goods would be treated equally; the 'blind spot' just above Utility prices would be eliminated, and there would be no loss of revenue if Utility schemes were extended to other products. There was a risk that supplies might become short on the home market, although Wilson thought that public demand would be likely to ensure the continued manufacture, under a 'D' scheme, of an adequate supply of goods of Utility quality; if not, he added that he would be willing 'to take separate action to secure their provision', although what that action could be was unclear.[28]

The report of the Douglas Committee (Cmnd 8452), published in February 1952, rehearsed the benefits and disadvantages of Utility. Its central conclusion was that to remove discrimination against imports, get the Government off the GATT hook and avoid the 'blind spot', the link between Utility and tax exemption had to be changed. Tax exemption should be linked to value, with tax charged only on the excess over the determined value – in other words, the 'D' scheme. There were some inconsistencies or anomalies for which the circumstances of the report's appearance probably accounted. It generally took on trust industry's argument that, except in a seller's market, manufacturers would be bound to produce the good value, sound quality and low priced goods which consumers demanded and which Utility had typified. But this confidence overlooked the experience of the 1920s and 1930s when poor quality and poor value goods abounded; the possibility that many manufacturers would always choose short-term profit over long-term reputation was ignored. The committee also appeared illogical in recommending that separate arrangements should be made for furniture, because of the need to protect the public from poor quality goods in that sector.

More important than any arguable flaws in the report, however, was the fact that it had been doubly up-staged by events. First, as we have seen, the preferred solution was already known. Secondly, the 1951 general election had swept away the Labour government, bringing in a Conservative administration which, certainly on the face of it, would favour financial over physical controls. Soon after the election Henry Strauss, the new Parliamentary Secretary to the Board of Trade, was listening sympathetically as the Light Clothing Federation argued that:

'The time had come to consider not whether the Utility scheme should be dismantled, but what part, if any, was worth preserving. The women of this country would get better value and more variety ... if these restrictive schedules were abolished.'[29]

As part of the Budget proposals, therefore, on 13 March 1952, the new President of the Board of Trade, Peter Thorneycroft, was able to turn the Douglas Committee's words to advantage and announce a deregulatory package. The Utility furniture scheme would remain for the time being, but over 100 orders governing Utility clothing and footwear would be revoked and powers taken to prevent misleading use of the Utility mark; significantly, the BSI would be given the job of policing this usage. Purchase Tax would be levied along 'D' scheme lines: in individual categories, about 50 per cent of goods would be tax-free; the remaining half, instead of suddenly jumping into the full tax bracket, would be subject to a gradually increasing amount of tax. Only furniture and nylon stockings would continue to be price controlled.

To retain some of the quality element of Utility, textile and clothing associations were to work with the BSI on a range of British Standards (originally announced as 'Utility series) to provide some guarantee of quality or performance: shrink resistance, colour fastness, shower resistance of raincoats and the precise wool content of fabrics were examples of the subjects to be covered. Finally, the Government would introduce legislation to amend the Merchandise Marks Act, widening the definition of trade description so that it would become an offence to misuse terms such as 'waterproof' or 'fade-resistant'. Thorneycroft presented the changes to the Commons:

'Most of the Utility schemes no longer justify the faith which many people still have in them as providing a guarantee of quality or of value for money. I believe that the best safeguard is the standard of the manufacturers and workers ... working in a competitive system and seeking to meet the demands of the consumers. The Board of Trade should encourage industries to apply minimum standards worked out in conjunction with the British Standards Institution, and ... these should be combined wherever ... possible with the registration of certification marks which will enable the consumer to know which goods comply with the standards.'

He reminded the House that the Douglas Committee had been appointed by the previous Government:

'If anybody wishes to accuse me of murdering the old Utility scheme, I should protest that I merely have the misfortune of being caught with the body'.[30]

Labour MPs expressed predictable indignation at Thorneycroft's announcement. While admitting that the Utility scheme had imperfections ('full of holes', said Marcus Dodds), they 'saw not the slightest reason why we should rob the lower income groups of some of the blessings still to be found in it'. Apart from the feared impact on prices, doubt was cast on the new arrangements to protect quality. Hervey Rhodes, who had been Parliamentary Secretary under Wilson and Shawcross, paid tribute to BoT officials who had 'so painstakingly and enthusiastically worked for the benefit of the consumer'. He disputed the suggestion of Thorneycroft (and Douglas), that Utility specifications, having been made more flexible, had resulted in lower average quality; flexible specification cloth accounted for only a small proportion of all deliveries (true enough at that stage, no doubt). And he quoted the example of Utility specification 1.005 (spun rayon cloth), 'one of the finest textile quality products of this country', alleging that:

'... manufacturers are already being asked to debase it. If a fine cloth like that is subject to debasement ... what about other more ordinary cloths?'[31]

Hervey Rhodes also brought into the open the relationship of Utility to power struggles within Whitehall: the Purchase Tax resolution proposed that '... there shall no longer be power to define the classes of goods affected by any such Treasury order [i.e. as to tax] by reference to marks the use of which the Board of Trade have power to regulate'. In other words, the Board of Trade had lost any direct power which it might have had to influence taxation and selling prices. Within Whitehall the ability to take the initiative is always worth something, and Rhodes made the most of what was apparently a technical change:

'The Treasury have been aiming for a long time to get other Departments under their thumb. ... The Douglas scheme suited the Treasury down to the ground. By removing the Utility scheme from its previous basis, the birth right of the Board of Trade has been sold, because [it] can no longer increase prices. The right hon. Gentleman [Thorneycroft] has to go to the Treasury and ask "Please can I do something about prices?" It is iniquitous that the Treasury can dominate a production Department'.[32]

The trade, and to some extent consumers, had been well prepared for the change; percentage margins on most Utility clothing had already been abolished in January, 1952, leaving only the maximum price control. Despite some confusion, for example about what would happen to existing stocks of Utility cloth, the *Drapers' Record* thought retailers must welcome the new freedom of action, while pointing out that it also signalled the final demise of the sellers' market. Consumers would also expect action, not just manufacturers' promises, on quality standards and marking. To most people the old tax-free/Utility link was simply replaced by a new low-price/tax-free link, although numerous anomalies remained under the new 'D' tax scheme. As a final farewell to Utility the *Drapers' Record* (8 March 1952) warned the Government that the new scheme had already created its own brand of 'D' scheme dodgers – retailers who would get the maker-up to invoice at a 'below-D' price and then accept an additional payment in cash. The retailer could then sell the goods tax-free. Plenty of work therefore remained for the Customs and Excise sleuths, to whom the editor wished 'good hunting'.

NOTES

1   Hargreaves and Gowing, 1951, p475–476.
2   Hennessy, 1992, p89.
3   Calder, 1969, p280.
4   Dorner, 1975, p9; Utility furniture underwent a similar change, with the introduction of three quality grades.
5   PRO, BT 64/213.
6   PRO, BT 64/243; a later suggestion, equally unsuccessful, was that Utility might apply only to so-called 'common user' goods such as sheets and towels, not to 'fashion goods' (PRO. BT 64/735).
7   PRO, BT 64/877.
8   Garland, 1983, p243.
9   Dorner, 1975, p28.
10 Phillips, 1963, p131; this chapter in Sissons and French's anthology gives a lively account of the New Look in Britain.
11 *Reynolds News* , Feb. 1948; Mrs Ridealgh, 'a robust grandmother with a North country background', says Pearson Phillips, gave a string of interviews to the popular press. She had been a BoT civil servant during the war, involved with the 'Make Do and Mend' campaign.
12 Beaton, 1954, p217.
13 Addison, 1985, p52.
14 M-OA, *Report on the New Look*, FR3095, March 1949.
15 HofC, Vol. 469, Col. 351.
16 HofC, Vol. 467, Col. 2678–2682; firms in this sector had already been angered by the form-filling introduced by the Statistics of Trade Act, 1947, which would eventually (1950) result in the first Census of Distribution.
17 Bernard, 1953, p90.
18 PRO, BT 64/735.
19 PRO, BT 64/742; the report, *Utility and the Public: an enquiry made for the Board of Trade*, by Kathleen Box, appeared in October 1950: CoI reference NS 159/DB 1309/1.
20 PRO, BT 64/768; BoT may have tended to write down work of another Department; there was also an eye on the next general election. Sympathizing with the concerns of Customs and Excise, a senior official, signing himself merely 'R', minuted ponderously, in July 1950: 'To know that Customs are "uneasy" and "curious" reminds me. This sign which at the moment is no

bigger "Than a man's hand" will lead to joy in Israel. I would remind the Sec[retary] that my mind dwells very often on the lines of a Lancashire poet. "Owd time he's a troublesome codger. He keeps nudging us on to decay. An' whispers 'Th'art nobbut a lodger. Get ready for going away'" (PRO, BT 64/735).

21 Warwick, TUC annual reports.

22 HofC, Vol. 474, Cols. 360–361; Wilson was already embroiled with the manufacturers over the Clothing Industry Development Council, set up at the beginning of the year under the Industrial Organisation and Development Act, 1947. All firms were required to register with the Council, which had a wide general remit to promote research, improve design, stimulate exports, collect statistics and initiate education and training. The Council and the proposed levy on the industry which was supposed to support it were immediately challenged in the courts by sectors of the clothing industry. It was wound up in 1952 (PRO, BT 15/380, 15/339).

23 *The Times*, 8 Oct. 1951.

24 PRO, T233/630.

25 Warwick, MSS 222.

26 PRO, T233/630.

27 PRO, T233/629.

28 Ibid.

29 *The Times*, 30 Nov. 1951.

30 HofC, Vol. 497 Cols 1577 et seq. The 'D' scheme had a shorter life than the Utility it replaced; in 1955 it was in turn replaced by a flat rate of 5 per cent Purchase Tax on adult clothing;children's clothes remained exempt. The Douglas Committee, although precluded from recommending a flat rate tax, had clearly thought that it was the real solution.

31 HofC, Vol. 497, Col. 1652.

32 Ibid.

CHAPTER 6

Conclusions

'Designers ... wanted a bit of a razzle – or Binge – after
being forced for five years to keep to the official
specifications of Austerity.'

Bevis Hillier, *Austerity Binge*, 1975

'C'est en dernier ressort l'èsprit civique de la population
anglaise qui explique le succès du Système Utility comme
il explique le succès de la guerre.'

Bernard, 'Le Système Utility', 1953

Earlier chapters of this book have confirmed how widely Utility
clothes, boots and shoes, along with rationing and the other civilian
clothing controls, have featured in both learned and popular accounts
of the Second World War. The volume of the official history by
Hargreaves and Gowing and work by economic commentators such as
Cairncross include some analysis, explicit or implicit, of the way
Utility (and other controls) affected UK prices, production and
distribution. Two substantial contemporary studies, one English (H.
E. Wadsworth)[1] and one French (Jean-René Bernard)[2], looked in some
detail at the pros and cons of Utility; Harriet Dover's more recent
work[3] discusses the particular legacy of Utility furniture.

Taking account of all these sources it is possible to look at the
'success' of Utility from a number of angles. First, did the schemes do
the job the Government wanted? Did they help make efficient use of
raw materials, keep prices down, and assure an equitable distribution
of civilian clothing? Secondly, did Utility and the other civilian
clothing measures have any effect on morale; do we believe that they
helped prevent the kind of civil unrest which the politicians
remembered from 1917–1918?

In the longer term, did the Utility schemes have any effect on the
efficiency or profitability of manufacturers or retailers? Were Utility
clothing designs and styles merely a wartime aberration, or can they
be seen to fit into a broader sweep of 20th-century fashion? Did the
kind of collaboration between Government and industry which Utility

exemplified catch on? Is there some inconsistency between the greatly increased efficiency of firms in wartime and the continued poor performance of British industry, relative to our major competitors, today? Finally, can we conceive of a Utility-type scheme succeeding at other times, or in other countries?

Wadsworth started his 1948 essay by saying that the Utility scheme was 'entirely new and indigenous'; it owed nothing to control devices in other countries and, he thought, had never been copied. He was not entirely accurate: the Utility scheme as it eventually emerged could be said to be unique, but it is not difficult to identify its origins in the short-lived and partial 'standard' clothing experiments of 1918. And, as well as the enquiries made by the South African and other governments, schemes similar to Utility were actually essayed in France both during and immediately after the war; these are described by Bernard.

Under the German occupation the French administration first instructed industry to produce certain basic items of furniture for sale only to those whose homes had been damaged by enemy action. Later, in 1943–1944, furniture companies were asked to produce a range of 'priority' furnishings; the main aim was to reduce the extent to which French factories and machinery were closed down or removed to Germany. After the liberation of France these schemes were replaced by one for providing basic furniture known as *Meubles de France* which, unlike Utility, was voluntary: manufacturers were not compelled to produce any of these goods. Then, in 1946, legislation was passed giving the Ministry of Industrial Production powers to devise programmes *d'utilité sociale*. Although, according to Bernard, these powers were never used directly, the French government did influence manufacturers through its power to allocate raw materials. The French schemes, however, which applied to selected sectors, including some textiles and baby carriages, only faintly echoed the British Utility model. Everything hinged on voluntary collaboration between manufacturers and ministry; those who agreed to reduce profit margins got preference in allocation of raw materials, tools and machinery in order to produce the *articles utilitaires*; some branches of the textile industry agreed that 50 per cent of factory output would be goods of this kind. Small firms could gain even more, by way of tax concessions.

Bernard concludes that the French programmes had minimal impact; in textiles and clothing the amounts produced were insufficient and 'almost ridiculous'. Most textile and footwear firms refused to collaborate; the programmes lasted only a couple of years, and the government's first priority was to favour small manufacturers and shopkeepers rather than to influence the overall supply and price of clothing, as in Britain.

By contrast, in Britain, although it is not easy to separate out the peculiar impact of Utility, all accounts agree that, in their totality, the civilian clothing measures had substantial and beneficial effects. They ensured a continuous supply of civilian clothes and shoes in most of the categories, sizes and qualities which people wanted – with the kind of conspicuous exceptions we have noted: Wellington boots, fully-fashioned stockings, children's wear. The Government's prime aim was achieved: the price of clothing and the cost of living index were kept down; 'Owing largely to the Utility scheme', say Hargreaves and Gowing, the index of clothing prices, which in April 1942 stood at 195 (the general index about 130), fell to 164 by the end of 1943. At a corresponding period in the First World War the index had reached 260 compared with pre-war levels.

Table 6.1   Cost of living index

	Clothing	All items
Sept. 1939	100	100
June 1940	137	117
May 1941	177	129
June 1942*	195	128
June 1943	168	128
June 1944	165	129
June 1945	167	132

* Purchase Tax remitted Sept. 1942
Source:Hargreaves and Gowing p648.

Table 6.1 illustrates the changing relationship between the cost of living index as a whole and its clothing component. It is worth bearing in mind that too steep a fall in the cost of living index would have been as embarrassing to the Treasury as too rapid a rise, since it would have led, theoretically, to calls for reductions in wages. Maintaining

Utility and other controls from 1945 onwards prevented the rapid price escalation seen after the First World War when, by June 1920, the index had risen to 330. Concern that this would happen again was emerging by 1944 when, in a Supply Committee debate, Ellis Smith MP (Labour, Stoke) urged that Utility should be kept, post war:

'... if we are to avoid that inflation, of which some of us live in dread because of the experience we had in the Army of Occupation after the last war, I think a certain amount of this [Utility] policy should be carried on after the war, in order that we can provide our people with furniture and household goods of good quality at minimum prices'.[4]

As before, we need to keep worries about Utility, however genuine, in perspective. Clothing and footwear, although essential to the civilian population, represent only a minor part of their purchases in any one year; by 1953, immediately after the abolition of Utility, average household expenditure on clothing ranged from 4/6 (23p) to 77/8 (£3.88) per week, depending on household income, and represented between 7–14 per cent of total household expenditure. By 1956 aggregate UK consumer expenditure on clothing had still only reached 113 per cent of its 1938 level, rather below the increase of 115 per cent for all such expenditure.[5]

In the winter of 1943–1944 Treasury and Board of Trade officials undertook a study into Utility schemes and the cost of living; their aim was to find out how much each of the cost components – raw materials, wages, distribution costs and others – had contributed to the overall increase in the price of manufactured goods. The study found that increases ranged between 50 and 75 per cent for all factors. Board of Trade officials found 'sinister' the relatively high rate of increase for 'other items', which included profits. A number of explanations suggest themselves: firms would have faced additional overheads, for example, because of the cost of caring for non-productive (non-nucleus) plant. The study prophesied, fairly if unimaginatively, that:

'... clothing prices should not rise after the war, and may even fall slightly for a time provided that existing controls are maintained, that raw material prices and the cost of living index are kept reasonably stable, and that the margin between the increase in wages and the increase in the cost of living does not materially widen'.[6]

The study at least endorsed the intuitive feeling that Utility was helping to keep prices down. Work of this kind, in which Hugh Gaitskell took part, and the more general experience of Utility and other controls, would have helped inform the attitude of the post-war Labour administration when Hugh Dalton, the arch-enthusiast for rationing, austerity and physical controls, moved to the Treasury. Dalton's biographer puts it that:

'Before the war Dalton had spoken and written much on the subject of planning. He did not abandon his earlier ideas. His view of planning did not greatly differ from the planning which already existed in the war economy. He believed that such planning should be extended and given a more radical purpose'.[7]

If all this would seem to perpetuate the negative, restrictive aspect of Utility, a more positive outcome was predicted by another temporary civil servant involved in the work, W. B. Reddaway, who foresaw continued improvements in efficiency in the clothing trade as, for example, more retailers adopted the practices of Marks and Spencer, and those from across the Atlantic. Some improvement in manufacturing efficiency could also be expected.

With the evidence still fresh, official historians concluded that Utility, the austerity rules, allocation of materials and concentration had all contributed to increased productivity in clothing and textiles. In the doubling and weaving sections of the cotton industry most manufacturers believed that efficiency had gone up by 10 to 15 per cent. In the wool industry long runs, predominantly of Utility cloths, had brought about productivity gains of up to 30 per cent. In the finishing industries firms were agreed on the large savings which resulted from receiving bulk orders from a smaller number of merchant converters; a spokesman for the yarn-dyeing trade said that pre-war labour and material costs in the industry had been disproportionately high because of the excess of small dyeing quantities needed to cope with the variety of shades in use: he looked forward to a continuation of the benefits of Utility.

Where garment makers too reported large productivity gains – as high as 75 per cent for individual firms – the austerity (style) restrictions may have been the main contributor, although the ISLFD's 'templates' for Utility fashions must have helped, as did the virtual elimination of fashion changes and the smoothing of seasonal trading achieved by rationing. In the hosiery and knitwear industries, again, simplification of garments and long runs meant increased efficiency for most firms; by the end of 1942 a labour force less than half that of pre-war days was handling 75 per cent of the pre-war volume of yarn. As a result it was possible, in 1944, to reduce maximum selling prices for some hosiery items.

Table 6.2 shows the change in numbers employed in textiles and clothing (aggregating several sectors) and in footwear:

Table 6.2 Numbers employed in Utility sectors

	1939 '000s	1945 '000s	change %
Textiles & clothing	1087	683	– 37
Footwear	135	95	– 29

Source: Hargreaves and Gowing, p641.

A smaller number of employees does not of itself imply greater efficiency; in many firms the younger, better skilled and more productive employees left, for example to join the armed forces, leaving less well-trained, older and less robust workers. Although Table 6.2 shows the change in footwear employment as around 30 per cent, the trade association (BFMF) claimed that nearly 50 per cent of the trained, pre-war workforce was lost, the difference being made up through employment of 'green' (untrained) labour, pensioners and women returners. There must therefore also have been improvements in production. In the cotton industry, for example, the more rigid (4-digit) Utility specifications introduced in 1942 were said to have brought about something like a revolution in the practice of Lancashire mills. Standard lines and consequent long runs accounted for about 80 per cent of home trade production. The Utility scheme proved that a variety of garments could be produced from a limited range of closely-specified cloths, with the Utility mark enabling tight price control, and also that continuous running and uniform quality could be achieved.[8]

Work on Utility also helped firmly to establish qualities such as fully-shrunk fabrics, crease-resistance and tests for fastness to light and washing. These qualities were not new. They had been evolved during the 1930s by the 'decadent, dilatory and virtually insolvent textile industry' (Wadsworth's ironic description). But the spread of good practice, the technique of quality control and the idea of the quality mark or label on cotton cloth were Utility's legacy to the post-war industry. The production of Utility specifications was effectively the BSI's first involvement in consumer protection; in 1942 the Government recognized the BSI as the sole organization for issuing national standards, an aspect of the Institution's work which grew enormously in scope and importance. Work on textile standards led to the establishment of BSI's textile branch in Manchester in 1947 and also probably contributed to the setting up of the Women's Advisory Committee in 1951. Although all of these developments might well have come about in any case, it seems clear that the link with Utility speeded them up.[9]

Wadsworth's considered view was that Utility had ensured the availability of civilian clothing 'probably more durable and possibly cheaper than was possessed by any other belligerent'. In the longer term the scheme had bequeathed the cotton industry:

'... certain improvements on common pre-war practice [for example] the elimination of excessive filling materials ... and prescribed full shrinkage for all heavy overall cloths. It set high standards of waterproofness for gaberdines. In rayons the outstanding feature was ... the prescription of crease-resist finishes.'[10]

By no means all firms gained: where skilled craftsmen were lost standards lapsed, producers and consumers alike accepting second best. In the longer term, the enervating experience of the sellers' market eventually made it more difficult for British firms to compete successfully against foreign competitors. Lack of any spur to innovate, to create new products, was a depressing consequence of Utility and the austerity rules. Quantifying the benefits and disadvantages which British industry inherited from Utility and other controls and then striking a balance between them is therefore a daunting task. Indeed, Stephen Broadberry[11] argues that such an exercise would have little point since 'the direct effects of war on the British economy do not account for much of the subsequent disparities in economic performance'. Accepting that the main feature of British manufacturing industry in the decades since 1950 has been its decline, not absolute but relative to our competitors, there is a general consensus that the root causes pre-date both of the world wars.

Corelli Barnett[12] is one of many who trace the origins of Britain's relative industrial decline to the mid-Victorian era when 'the most important – decisive – contribution of the European states to their countries' industrial progress lay in elaborate and coherent systems of national education'. Barnett also blames the insistence of the wartime coalition and the post-war Labour government on building the 'new Jerusalem' for the poor performance of the British economy. But Cairncross, a less abrasive commentator, discounts this; further, he argues that the post-war government's freedom of action was heavily constrained by unavoidable problems – how to pay for imports, how to earn dollars, how to run down the armed forces, and so on. He also points out that, although Labour politicians like Dalton might publicly espouse the concept of planning, the physical controls inherited from the war, were by no means all-embracing and were already being phased out as the war ended (although they did have some effect in restraining demand at home and resisting inflation). As Harold Wilson's politically motivated 'bonfire of controls' illustrates, the post-war government in Britain was far from wholehearted in its pursuit of economic planning; there was 'much talk of planning,' writes Cairncross, 'but no published plan. The economy moved from one economic crisis to another in a way that seemed to make nonsense of the idea that it was planned.'[13]

Underlying all the factors, such as poor education as identified by Barnett, Peter Hennessy suggests that the true weakness of the post-war industrial scene was a combination of the long sellers' market and the fatal complacency which characterized a large number – perhaps a majority – of British industrialists and bureaucrats:

'... a hydra headed monster with limbs spread far beyond the production line. Thanks to the war Britain's exporters could sell virtually anything they could make, while the world re-equipped and the Germans and the Japanese picked themselves up off the floor. The longer term structural weakness of the British industrial base was deeply concealed under the satisfactions of a tremendous performance under conditions of war and a rapid regaining of pre-war export levels.'[14]

It is neither fanciful nor entirely a matter of hindsight to find some of this exemplified in the cotton industry. Wadsworth, while anticipating the Douglas Committee's view that Utility could operate only as a short-term measure, believed not only that it had performed its main job of price control 'tolerably well', but in addition that Utility had been a 'valuable experience for the [cotton] industry; it has swept away a good deal of mediocre stuff (together, no doubt, with a few pearls)'.[15] But when Dalton, four years earlier, in 1944, reviewed the industry, he was pessimistic; where Wadsworth wrote hopefully of innovations, increased productivity and the experience gained from long runs of Utility cloth, Dalton saw 'obsolescent machinery and an out of date form of organisation' with 60 to 70 per cent of the industry's buildings and much of the machinery dating from the 19th century.

What was worse, said Dalton, was that most cotton manufacturers 'showed no appreciation of the need for reorganisation and re-equipment'.[16] In May 1952, the month which saw the final demise of Utility, the chairman of the Cotton Board, Sir Raymond Streat, explained that the cotton trade was not suffering from a major slump but from a depression caused by 'mass emotion' in the markets, which would soon be corrected by 'painful adjustments'; that is, reductions in capacity which would not repeat the 'maladjustments' of the wartime concentration scheme.[17] Encouraging noises like this, however, could not conceal the fact that the decline in British cotton had only been slowed, not reversed, first by the introduction of tariffs, then by wartime service and Utility production. After the war, propaganda and recruitment campaigns ('Britain's Bread Hangs by Lancashire's Thread') were accompanied by some improvements in layout and use of machinery, but British mills still lagged behind American in terms of automatic looms and the new ring-spinning techniques.

Rather oddly, perhaps, in view of the many unkind comments from within the trade reported in earlier chapters, fashion industry spokesmen were later among Utility's warmer supporters. The verdict of Frederick Starke, director of the wholesalers A. Starke & Co., quoted by Elizabeth Ewing, was that:

'The geniuses who invented the Utility scheme had a great say in the development of the fashion industry. Although fashion [was] slowed down by restriction it emerged with a structure which, so far as manufacturing was concerned, was better than pre-war.'[18]

Reasons suggested for this improvement in fashion production included tight control of raw materials and prices, compelling manufacturers to choose cloth more carefully. Standards of manufacture were also controlled; wartime necessity meant that the public demanded long-lasting well made clothes. Further, garment-makers were forced, in many cases for the first time (save for those who had already tasted the discipline of relationships with buyers such as Marks and Spencer), to take seriously the costing of their work. The Apparel and Fashion Industry Association (AFIA), whose secretary, Herbert Goodier, wrote a book on costing for the garment industry in 1946, concluded (in 1950) that

'A revolution has taken place behind the smoke-screen of wartime conditions. Laying down of Government specifications for cloth meant that this subject had to be given close attention by manufacturers who had to make themselves knowledgeable ... and buy judiciously.'[19]

The AFIA did not attribute all of the improvements to Utility; the concentration scheme, by no means universally welcomed at the time, had, they said, prevented the mushrooming of new speculative companies and so led to increased stability and efficiency in the industry. Experience gained in mass producing uniforms and Utility lines with maximum speed and minimum labour led to more scientific, better planned and mechanized methods in the clothing trade as a whole. It was even possible that the irritating restrictions on trimmings and ornaments not only simplified production but also had a 'beneficial effect on much of fashion'.

Perhaps, too, the Utility experiment may have helped, even if only marginally, to improve the place of the designer in the clothing industry. As in footwear, design generally had a low status in the British clothing industry of the 1930s. In 1937 the Council for Art and Industry set up a dress committee. The chairman was the ubiquitous Fred Marquis; other committee members included James Laver, Alison Settle, plus officials from the Board of Trade, Board of Education and

London County Council. The Committee's report, 'Design and Designer in the Dress Trade', re-published by HMSO in 1945, found that the UK fashion trade was losing out because of the lack of good design; there was little liaison between education authorities and industry: most training was directed at machinists. Rates of pay for designers in the clothing industry were low; art school graduates turned instead to journalism and advertising.

The committee believed that 'The importance of good design is no longer confined to the better end of the trade; ... an appreciation of design is now shared by all classes of women'. French manufacturers and those who made decisions on design in France had a 'better appreciation of what is good than their opposite numbers in this country'. The large imports of low-priced well-designed dresses from the US and Europe could only be matched by UK manufacturers 'if the designers are forthcoming and *the trade can be persuaded to employ them*' (emphasis added). One of the effects of Utility (and, of course, of the general scarcity of raw materials) was to enhance the importance of the designer in making the most economic use of each piece of cloth, a lesson that must have been learned by at least some of the manufacturers.

Elizabeth Ewing concludes that, taken together, Utility and its related controls produced a stability and prosperity which had previously been 'rare' in the fashion industry. From the Second World War date all the main features of present large-scale clothes production: large modern factories, planned production, the breakdown of manufacturing processes and the introduction of trained managers and technicians.[20]

In the retail trade, abolition of Utility in 1952 was generally welcomed; earlier chapters have illustrated the pressure which small shopkeepers felt themselves to be under from Utility, rationing and price control. If we may take Lord Woolton yet again as our source, Utility was equally irksome to the department stores. Returning to Lewis's after the Conservative election defeat in 1945, Woolton recalls asking a shop manager how he fixed the selling prices for coats, to be told that they came from a book published by the Board of Trade: 'I had spent many years trying to train managers to be merchants, and here I found them instructed by some regulation issued by Dr Dalton'.[21]

Yet, although the first issue of *Drapers' Record* that year headlined the expected end of Utility as 'A great start to 1952', the tone of its eventual obituary (12 April 1952) was more evenly balanced than one might have expected:

'By and large retailers did not fare badly under the old [price-controlled Utility] percentages, largely due to their being based on high cost prices and to the increased rate of stock turn when too much money was chasing too few goods. Competition then was virtually non-existent ... and expenses were reasonably low.'

The editor pointed out that although replacement of Utility by the 'D' scheme meant that traders had 'freedom of action', they would have to get used to seeing less money, also predicting that there would be strong public demand for some form of quality guarantee and more legislation on labelling. Eventually, too, the journal could foresee the emergence of another, and perhaps more frightening, bogey – the abolition of retail price maintenance.

If retailers in general were at best neutral, writers have perceived a more definite and lasting effect of Utility among the chain stores, above all in the case of Marks and Spencer. The writer of the company's centenary history, Asa Briggs, believes that the company benefited from the Utility scheme because Utility clothes, 'which closely followed Marks and Spencer's standard specifications', contributed the bulk of the company's turnover in this period and were exempt from Purchase Tax. By contrast, competitors, such as the department stores, had a higher proportion (although still only a minority) of sales among non-Utility, and taxable, goods.[22] An earlier M&S chronicler, Goronwy Rees, had summed up the impact of Utility thus:

'... the war helped, almost accidentally, to confirm the company in the correctness of the fundamental principles which underlay its merchandising policy.'[23]

What was seen as a specific benefit to Marks and Spencer was, of course, part of a much more general change in British retailing between, say, the 1930s and 1960s: the increasing power of chain stores in the high streets, the emphasis on labelled goods, guaranteed quality and value for money, close links between retailer and manufacturer, long runs, careful pre-planning and costing. After the Second World War, says Hopkins, the chain stores emerged as a:

'classless, efficient, decently functional, distributive model of the new age ... where the doctor's wife and docker's wife could ... avail themselves of the growing range and quality of mass-produced goods'[24]

At the other end of the scale, he adds, 'The little dressmaker of pre-war days had disappeared ... and would not be back'. It would be wrong to suggest that this change was not already on its way or that the chain stores won quite as overwhelming a victory as Hopkins suggests (even during the war the small, high quality non-Utility boutique survived in smart high street locations). But the Utility period saw a strengthening of trends already apparent in the 1930s. J. B. Jefferys, writing in 1954, listed factors which had contributed to the dominance of the multiples: shortage of labour (between 1938 and 1945 employment in distributive trades fell by 32 per cent, almost exactly the same as the drop in clothing and footwear manufacture); barriers to newcomers entering the field; working to fixed profit margins, and emphasis on standardization and organization. Well managed retailers, good at increasing turnover with fewer staff, did best. On some measures (numbers of stores opening, for example) progress may have been minimal:

'The war and immediate post-war years have been described as a period in which the developments in the structure and techniques of the distributive trades were few. In future, however, those years may be seen as marking the end of one phase of the history of the distributive trades and the beginning of another.'[25]

Jefferys's figures show that the multiples' share of trade in clothing and footwear, which had increased rapidly during the 1930s, continued to grow, albeit less significantly, between 1939 and 1950. He concluded that the wartime and post-war controls helped ensure that the future of retailing would lie in the 'further combination of experience and advantages of large-scale methods of distribution with the knowledge and techniques of large-scale production'.

Trying to isolate and quantify the outcome of the Utility schemes becomes even less of an exact science when we start to look at their effect on fashion in the sense of how clothes look, and on 'morale'. The social surveys carried out soon after the war (reported in Chapter 5) seemed to show that, with a little prompting, many people were generally in favour of Utility. But the surveys also indicated that what people liked best were guaranteed low prices, rather than other qualities inherent in Utility goods. The Douglas Committee report concluded that most people had only a vague idea of the link between the Utility mark and guaranteed quality. By the time the Douglas report appeared, of course, it was politic to play down the importance of the Utility mark; the report suggested that all would be well if choice were widened (and perhaps the Merchandise Marks Act strengthened). But the original aim of Utility, to provide essential goods of guaranteed quality, had been diluted. If proof were needed that its main appeal did not lie in the design of the clothes themselves, then the coming of the New Look in 1947 provides it. Those who had the money – and coupons – to make a choice, voted for change. The 'New Look' dresses in the shops may have looked less dramatic than the original Dior creations, but there was nevertheless a notable change in skirt length and other basic design features. The care lavished by Digby Morton and other ISLFD members on the Utility creations, and the publicity generated for them by the Government public relations machine, could no more make them permanent than any other product of the fashion industry. Similarly in the furniture industry, once the Utility and other controls were lifted, the *Architectural Review* predicted that people would ignore the best efforts of Gordon Russell and his disciples to educate them in favour of 'honesty of design':

> 'As long as most furniture looks as austere and institutional as the Board of Trade's, the majority of forced purchasers will ... return to the wildly grained H.P. walnut suite with stuck-on moulded ornaments.'[26]

During the war the press had taken the line that simplicity and lack of colour were what people wanted. However, the quotation at the head of this chapter (from Bevis Hillier's work on the demise of austerity) suggests that by the late 1940s people were ready for a change. Mass Observation, which carried out a survey at the time of the Council of Industrial Design's 'Britain Can Make It' exhibition in 1946, concluded that the British public wanted 'more excitement, decoration and fun' than they were being offered. The survey highlighted the gap between the 'essentially paternalistic middle class attitudes' of the design establishment, and the desires and aspirations of the public.[27]

Just as it is wrong to see the New Look eclipsing Utility at a stroke, so it is wrong to attribute too fundamental a role to Utility. When Hopkins, in his eponymous history of the New Look, argues that Utility, by insisting on good simple design and by specifying materials, made it difficult to cover up 'shoddiness' in clothes and furniture with 'mouldings or trimmings', he ignores both the evidence that many people clearly liked those trimmings and that, in any event, shortage of raw materials would have pushed manufacturers in the same direction.

Rather than seeing it as an attempt by the 'design establishment' to force a switch of direction on a reluctant public, it is more helpful to look at Utility fashion as one strand in longer term social change, say from the Edwardian to the Elizabethan periods of the 20th century. In that sense rationing, uniforms, Utility and austerity can all be viewed as allies in a continuing campaign. Madge Garland, in particular, although writing about women's uniforms, could equally have been describing the impact of low priced, good quality Utility clothes:

'... for the first time in history fashion (such as it was) derived from the proletariat, not from the privileged [and] a vast number of lower-class women who were drafted into the services experienced the discipline of good dressing and the feel of what were comparatively good clothes.'[28]

Looking at fashion in this social, rather than aesthetic, way supports the argument that Utility and the New Look of 1947 were not opposites, but examples of the same trend – the spread of 'fashion' to an ever-widening market – a market served by the chain stores:

'After the war fashion became the concern of all. Instead of being exclusive it had to satisfy the tastes of millions who were as much, if not more, interested in whether their clothes were light and comfortable, easy to wash and care for, as in whether their style was the exclusive possession of a privileged few.'[29]

The more plausible legacy of Utility is therefore economic rather than aesthetic. It is easy to think of the fashion business as a pyramid: a handful of artistic geniuses at the peak, with a larger number of manufacturers and distributors simply waiting to translate their creations into goods for sale to the mass market at the base of the pyramid. But this top-down analysis is insufficient; one of the simpler passages in Walker's *Design History and the History of Design* describes style as follows:

> 'A successful style involves the convergence of the tastes of both designers and consumers. It is the result of a complex combination of factors [only] one of which is the current aesthetic situation.'[30]

In the garment industry change is endemic and (despite the temptation to see regular cycles in such phenomena as skirt-length) unpredictable;[31] it is linked not only to the creativity of the designer but to technical developments and changes in the way people live and work. Fashion designers and those associated with them, including the fashion media, need to have change in the same way that artists need to create new work, to show that they have ideas: that is what they are paid for. Manufacturers and distributors of cloth and clothing need change in order to create sales and, if possible, to replace cheaper lines with more expensive ones, increasing profits and creating growth. Consumers need change because, in the end, garments have to be replaced and because clothes have social or aesthetic values as well as practical ones and because populations change in terms of age and activities; clothes that were practical and comfortable for office, factory or ARP post in 1942 will not serve for the disco, the jogging track or the Job Club in 1995.

Occupying the middle of the pyramid, retailers have to be alive to the talents of designers, the changing needs and fortunes of the consumer and also the technical capability of producers of raw materials and garments across the world. The great strength of Marks and Spencer (and other chain stores) may be put down to their ability to carry out this juggling act successfully. Indeed, some critics now argue that the British textile trade has suffered from this strength: firms prefer to take a bulk order from Marks and Spencer for a safe and tested fabric, rather than experiment with original and adventurous materials and shorter runs. Hence, the argument goes, the more innovative fashion designers will buy fabrics from Italy, where a number of smaller manufacturers specialize in shorter runs and greater variety. But Marks and Spencer, too, has to adapt, looking for more innovation and installing changing rooms to replace the old 'quality guaranteed and goods always exchanged' policy.

So it is wrong to think of changes in fashion as somehow being imposed on an unwilling market by the designers or their lackeys in the fashion press. Equally, it would be wrong to imagine that consumers, by some act of collective will, regularly alter style, although in the long term it is their ability to pay for clothes that meet their needs which influences trends (possibly, too, consumers can kill off a fashion idea which they do *not* like).Although few would have admitted to liking it, Utility was not a radical switch of direction; the Government, with the help of fashion designers and to suit its own purposes, nudged forward relatively minor changes in the way men's and women's clothes looked, the kind of incremental change with which all elements of the clothing pyramid could live.

The successful partnership between designer and manufacturer represented by Utility, however, was not enough to ensure permanent success for the British fashion business. In 1993 national newspapers were running features which began by praising British designers: 'No other country begins to rival in quantity or quality Britain's provision of opportunities for the young to train as designers,'[32] but went on to point out that Britain's domestic market is too small to support their efforts; young British designers are snapped up by design houses in other parts of Europe. British manufacturers and designers are accused of being unable or unwilling to work together: 'British designers have blamed UK manufacturers' conservatism, while manufacturers blamed designers for a lack of realism'.[33] Finally, critics still write about the 'astonishing post-war lethargy' in the British textile industry, which did not invest in new plant or technology.

If there is an aspect even less tangible than that of fashion, it must be the impact of Utility on morale. We can hardly take, as a starting point, the idea that the act of buying clothes and shoes labelled Utility in itself improved civilian morale and made people feel better during the Second World War (although, 40 or so years on, it was possible to find people who gloried in the long wear provided by a Utility bed or even a Utility dress – the latter perhaps in its umpteenth incarnation as a pet's blanket). Utility's relation to morale is perhaps best described as second-hand; it contributed not only to the visibly stable cost of living, but to the unquantifiable feeling of shared sacrifice – the 'conspicuous fairness' which Peter Hennessy, and the introduction to this book suggest was indispensable to public acceptance of institutionalized privation.[34]

The awkward question is, of course, how can we be sure? Why is there this consensus among historians that people started to feel and behave differently during the 1940s? Of course it sounds plausible that measures like rationing, Utility and conscription, which people could see applied universally, might accompany a change to a more 'collectivist and egalitarian' society.[35] Some writers go further, arguing that wartime solidarity helped bring about a more lasting change in British society and in politics, more substantial than the changes which flowed from the First World War. John Stevenson, for example, believes that 'In a number of respects the second world war left a more permanent mark upon British society than the first', yet even he admits that 'Debate continues ... as to how profound the changes were, and how far the war was responsible for them'.[36] By contrast, Henry Pelling argues that the Second War actually caused *less* psychological shock to society because the 'major institutions all emerged ... basically unaltered'.[37]

Yet danger and privation were so widespread, shortages of essential goods so severe and unpredictable, recent social and political history so divisive, that it is hard to dispute that measures of 'conspicuous fairness' like Utility were right – and politicians like Churchill wrong to oppose them. Without such measures, social and industrial unrest *might* have been no worse than in the event they were, but this was a risk which the Government could not take. One of the few quantifiable measures of civilian discontent – numbers of industrial disputes – seems to confirm this judgement. In 1915–1918 the number of days lost in industry each year through stoppages averaged 4.2 million; in 1939–1945 the average was 1.9 million (as an even greater contrast, in 1919–1921 the figure had been 49.1 million).[38] We may even think that the general tone of industrial relations was less strident in the Second World War: as in 1914–1918, there was continual discontent among coal miners, for example because of the superior wages offered to munitions workers. Yet Hugh Dalton records the rapturous applause which an audience of miners (by no means a Churchillian constituency) gave the Prime Minister at the Central

Hall, Westminster, in December 1942.[39]

Is it possible to envisage a Utility scheme in other circumstances either in Britain or elsewhere? Had Labour, rather than the Conservatives, won the election of October 1951, would Utility have somehow survived, accompanied rather than replaced by the 'D' scheme? Almost certainly Labour would have continued subsidies, through tax relief, on a wider range of goods. Perhaps Harold Wilson's plan for tougher consumer legislation would have built on the Utility mark. But the increasing trade in all sorts of goods across frontiers had destroyed one of the prime conditions for the acceptance of the Utility scheme – the virtually closed economy of wartime Britain.

Bernard's conclusions, published in 1953, remain difficult to fault today. For a Utility scheme to be successful he identifies three essential conditions: shortages of material and labour throughout the (closed) economy; acceptance of need by both producers and consumers; collaboration between public and private sectors. Only under the threat of war, he argues, would such collaboration be forthcoming; without it, the detailed specifications and regulation of Utility would be impossible: '... la mise sur pied de spécification est la base de toute la législation Utility'.[40]

Bernard goes on to adduce an interesting, if less compelling, reason why Utility succeeded in Britain, but not in France. Not only were the three basic preconditions lacking in France (more particularly after the war), he argues, but French society would *always* lack the necessary 'spirit of civic cooperation', the kind of tradition which, Bernard believes, has to underpin successful collaboration of public and private sectors. He elaborates on this by drawing a distinction between *representative* bodies (for example the British trade associations who worked on Utility) and *representational* ones where the interests represented expect to have continuing influence on political decisions; this he judges to be the norm in France. It is true that both in Bernard's day and today one can see differences between France and Britain in the representation of trade and other special interests. How much they contributed to the relative success of Utility in the one, and failure in the other, seems impossible of proof.

We do not, however, need to embrace what may seem Bernard's quaintly Anglophile views to accept his favourable verdict on Utility.

Nor do we need to agree with Wadsworth's claim that Utility was, like the Virgin birth, unprecedented and unparalleled. Nor, finally, must we accept at face value the praise which post-war Labour politicians heaped on the schemes while their officials were penning politely sceptical minutes to each other.

The Utility cloth, clothing and footwear schemes did the job which the Government wanted done. Despite the elaborate, often amended and irritating specifications and price lists, Utility was a key element in ensuring that reasonable supplies were available in the shops throughout the war; the quality and appearance of goods were at least tolerable and, for example in the case of footwear and much children's wear, better than the equivalent pre-war product. Above all, prices remained stable. Utility, concentration and the other measures were not powerful, long-lived or comprehensive enough to bring about any permanent improvement in the performance of Britain's manufacturing as a whole; in some sectors, however, and certainly in many firms, Utility was demonstrably helpful. On balance Utility probably did more good than harm to industry, helping to improve efficiency and productivity. In retailing, in the design of clothes and shoes, and in the development of the fashion industry, Utility worked with the grain, not against it.

So far as the public was concerned Utility clothes, like mothers-in-law and Wigan, became an easy target among music hall comedians ('Heard about the poor Utility girl? She's single-breasted'). Home Intelligence and Mass Observation reports might provide a wealth of less risqué but equally derogatory comment (more accurate, too: the ban on the double-breasted style applied not just to Utility but to all coats). But there are no records of civilians going naked rather than wear Utility, nor being rejected for the services because they lacked underwear. Nobody rioted, went on strike or smashed shop windows because they didn't like the look of Utility clothes. Even after 15 years of Utility and austerity, the dress torn from the back of the model in the rue Lepic was not the despised Utility, but the Dior creation.

NOTES

1   Wadsworth, 'Utility Cloth and Clothing Scheme' in *Review of*

Economic Studies Vol. XVI, Pt 2.40, 1948.

2   Bernard, 'Le Système Utility' in *Cahiers de la Fondation des Sciences Politiques*, No. 46, 1953.

3   Dover, *Home Front Furniture*, 1991.

4   HofC, Vol. 403, Col. 2692.

5   Carr-Saunders et al., 1958, pp158–162.

6   PRO, BT64/177.

7   Pimlott, 1985, p367.

8   Wadsworth, 1948, p95; the beneficial effects were not confined to cotton cloth manufacture: Pollard (*Development of the British Economy 1914–1967*) points out that the pressures of wartime production made most manufacturers more receptive to ideas of scientific and technological change. New methods of mass production, design and quality control and management were evolved. Productivity in manufacturing, as measured by the Census of Production's index of output per employee, showed an across-the-board increase of nearly 20 per cent between 1935 and 1948.

9   Eventually, with the end of Utility, BoT agreed a programme of co-operation with BSI and trade associations according to which BSI would take over about 50 former Utility specifications for cotton cloth, the registration of all Utility bedding specifications, and production of performance tests to guarantee colour fastness and non-shrinkage for rayon cloths. Dealing with wool cloths was considered too difficult

10 Wadsworth, 1948, p95.

11 Broadberry, 1988 *passim*.

12 In works such as *The Collapse of British Power*, 1972 and *The Audit of War* 1986.

13 Cairncross, 1992 *passim*; the long-term nature of Britain's problems was emphasized yet again in 1993: giving the annual Keynes Lecture, Professor S J Prais said that Britain's economic prosperity is still threatened by low education standards and inadequate vocational training (Prais: *Economic Performance and Education: the Nature of Britain's Deficiencies*, NIESR mimeo 1993).

14 Hennessy, 1992, p429.

15 Wadsworth, 1948, p94.

16 PRO, CAB 87/15, quoted in Barnett, 1986, p57.

17 *Financial Times*, 5 May 1952.

18 Ewing, 1974, p145.

19 *AFIA report*, 1950, quoted in Ewing, 1974, p147.

20 Ibid.

21 Woolton, 1959, p103; Woolton also remembered worrying that, under post-war controls, the 'good tempered tolerance of British people might well lead them to become a servile state'.

22 Briggs, 1973, p55. There is a puzzle here: Briggs's own account also shows that the proportion of Marks and Spencer's turnover accounted for by textiles of all kinds actually fell during the Utility period (1943–1948) to 69 per cent compared with 80 per cent both earlier (1938) and later (1953); the kinship between Government-imposed Utility and Marks and Spencer's success with good quality mass-market clothing remains more solidly based: the company would hardly draw attention to this relationship unless it reflected well on its own products.

23 Rees, 1973, p172.

24 Hopkins, 1963, p96.

25 Jefferys, 1954, p118; writing about a period before Census of Distribution statistics were available, Jefferys had to use a range of sources to estimate total numbers of retailers and their share of trade, including trade directories, company accounts and White Papers on National Income and Expenditure. His work documents the rise and rise of the multiples, including the 'variety' stores such as Marks and Spencer and British Home Stores, whose outlets almost doubled between 1935 and 1950.

26 *Architectural Review*, Jan. 1943; in 1993 the Furniture Industry Research Association (FIRA) found that nearly 50 per cent of UK purchases of living room and dining room furniture was still accounted for by 'traditional' or 'reproduction' designs. Harriet Dover points out that if high street retailers were pilloried by design reformers for being unadventurous, failing to encourage 1950's shoppers to refurnish in a 'contemporary' style, they had good reason for their caution: much furniture was bought on hire purchase, the retailer's money was tied up in the deal, and he could not risk dissatisfaction with novel designs.

27 M-OA, 244.

28 Garland, 1983, p244.

29 Rees, 1973, p172.

30 Walker, 1989, p164.

31 Docherty and Hann, 1993, p227; I am indebted to Dr Hann, Senior Lecturer in Textile Design & Management, University of Leeds, for drawing my attention to this and other papers on the

subject of stylistic change in womenswear products. The careful analyses which he and his collaborators have done convinces me, at least, that 'contrary to expectations ... regular and recurring fashion cycles are not evident'.

32 *Sunday Times* (Brenda Polan), 7 March 1993.
33 *Independent on Sunday* (Roger Tredre), 23 May 1993.
34 Hennessy, 1992, p50.
35 Addison, 1992, p327.
36 Stevenson, 1984, p460.
37 Pelling, 1970, p265.
38 CSO, 1951, p34; Taylor, 1965, p40.
39 Dalton, 1986, p529; Dalton, as a Durham MP, would naturally write warmly about coal miners, but there is no reason why, in his diaries, he should have bothered to flatter Churchill.
40 Bernard, 1953, p95.

APPENDIX

Biographical Notes

Many of the politicians and public figures mentioned in the text are so well known as to need no further identification; these brief notes are provided for ease of reference and are not intended to be definitive.

Sir William Maxwell (Max) Aitken, Baron Beaverbrook (1879–1964). Canadian newspaper owner. Conservative MP Ashton under Lyne 1910-16, Chancellor of Duchy of Lancaster and Minister of Information 1918–19, Minister of Aircraft Production 1940-41, Minister of State 1941, Minister of Supply 1941–42, Minister of War Production 1942, Lord Privy Seal 1943–45.

Sir Thomas Barlow (1883–1964). Director General of Civilian Clothing 1941–45, Chairman of District Bank Ltd. and Barlow and Jones Ltd.

Neville Chamberlain (1869–1940). Lord Mayor Birmingham 1915–16. Director General of National Service 1916–17. Unionist MP Birmingham Ladywood 1918–29, Edgbaston 1929–40. Postmaster General 1922–23, Paymaster General 1923, Minister of Health 1923, 1924–29, 1931. Chancellor of Exchequer 1923–24, 1931–37. Prime Minister 1937–40.

Sir Henry 'Chips' Channon (1897–1958). Diarist. Conservative MP Southend on Sea 1935–50, Southend West 1950-58. Parliamentary Private Secretary to R. A. Butler as Under Secretary of State for Foreign Affairs 1938–41.

Winston S. Churchill, later Sir Winston (1874–1965). MP (Liberal, then Conservative) Oldham 1900-1906, N W Manchester 1906–08, Dundee 1908–18, 1922, Epping 1924–45, Woodford 1945–64. President BoT 1908–10, Home Secretary 1910-11, First Lord of Admiralty 1911–15, 1939–40, Minister of Munitions 1917, Chancellor of Exchequer 1924–29, Prime Minister 1940–45, 1951–55.

Sir (Richard) Stafford Cripps (1889–1952). Labour MP East Bristol 1931–50, SE Bristol 1950. Solicitor General 1930-31, British Ambassador to USSR 1940–42, Lord Privy Seal and Leader of House of Commons 1942, Minister of Aircraft Production 1942–45, President BoT 1945–47, Minister of Economic Affairs 1947, Chancellor of Exchequer 1947–50.

Hugh Dalton, later Baron (1887–1962). Labour MP Peckham 1924–29, Bishop Auckland 1929–31, 1935–59. Under Secretary of State for Foreign Affairs 1929–31, Minister of Economic Warfare 1940–42, President BoT 1942–45, Chancellor of Exchequer 1945–47, Duchy of Lancaster 1948–50, Minister Town and Country Planning 1950-51, Local Government and Planning 1951.

Sir William Douglas (1890–1953). Civil servant 1914–51: HM Customs & Excise, Ministry of Labour, Department of Health for Scotland, HM Treasury, Ministry of Supply; Permanent Secretary Ministry of Health 1945–51. Later Chairman of Hospital for Sick Children, Great Ormond Street. Chaired Committee on Purchase Tax/Utility 1951–52.

Sir Andrew Duncan (1884–1952). Conservative MP City of London 1940-50. Minister of Supply 1940-41, 1942–45. President BoT 1940, 1941–42. Chairman of Iron and Steel Trades Confederation 1935–40, 1945–52.

Hugh Gaitskell (1906–63). Principal Private Secretary to Hugh Dalton, then Assistant Secretary, BoT, 1940-45. Labour MP S. Leeds 1945–63. Parliamentary Under Secretary Ministry of Fuel and Power 1946–47. Minister Fuel and Power 1947–50. Minister of State for Economic Affairs 1950. Chancellor of Exchequer 1950-51. Leader of Labour Party 1955–63.

Douglas Jay, later Baron (b 1907). Journalist. Assistant Secretary Ministry of Supply 1937–41. Principal Assistant Secretary BoT 1943–45. Personal Assistant to Prime Minister 1945–46. Labour MP North Battersea 1946–83. Parliamentary Private Secretary to Dalton (q.v.) as Chancellor of Exchequer 1947, Economic Secretary to Treasury 1947–50, Financial Secretary to Treasury 1950–51, President BoT 1964–67.

J. J. Llewellin, later Baron (1893–1957). Conservative MP Uxbridge 1929–45, Junior Minister 1939–41, Parliamentary Secretary Ministry of Transport 1941–42, President BoT 1942, Minister of Supply, resident in Washington, 1942–43, Minister of Food 1943–45.

Oliver Lyttleton, later Viscount Chandos (1893–1972). Conservative MP Aldershot 1940-54. President BoT 1940-41, 1945, Minister of State 1941–42, Minister of State Resident in Middle East 1942, Minister of Production 1942–44, Secretary of State for Colonies 1951–54.

Sir Frederick Marquis, Baron, later Earl, Woolton (1883–1964). Chairman Lewis's Ltd. Minister of Food 1940-43, Minister for Reconstruction 1943–45, Lord President of Council 1945, 1951–52, Chancellor of Duchy of Lancaster 1952–53, Minister of Materials 1953–54, Chairman of Conservative and Unionist Central Office 1946–55.

Sir Arnold Overton ('AEO')(1893–1975). Civil servant, Permanent Secretary BoT 1941–45, Ministry of Civil Aviation 1947–53. Reputedly cautious or negative, according to views of commentator;

Douglas Jay was said to walk the corridors of BoT chanting 'No No No, says A E O'. Dalton wrote: '... with a passive President, plus Overton, nothing would ever happen at BoT!'

W. B. Reddaway (b 1913). Lecturer, Reader, then Professor of Political Economy, Cambridge 1939–80 (then Emeritus Professor). Bank of England 1934–35. University of Melbourne 1936–37. Chief Statistician BoT 1940-47. Editor *Economic Journal* 1971–76. Consultant or economic adviser at times to OEEC, CBI, etc. Author of numerous books and articles.

Hervey Rhodes, later Baron R. of Saddleworth (1895–1987). Woollen manufacturer and local authority elected member. Labour MP Ashton-under-Lyne 1945–64. Parliamentary Private Secretary Minister of Pensions 1948–50, Parliamentary Secretary BoT 1950–51 and 1964–67.

Sir Hartley Shawcross, later Baron (b 1902). Barrister. Labour MP St Helens 1945–58. Attorney General 1945–51, President BoT 1951. Principal UK delegate to United Nations 1945–49. Chief UK prosecutor at Nuremberg war crimes trials 1945–46. Subsequently company director, Chairman Bar Council, Press Council, Chancellor Sussex University, etc.

Sir John Simon, later Viscount (1873–1954). Barrister. Liberal then Liberal National MP Walthamstow 1906–13, Spen Valley 1922–40. Solicitor General 1910–13, Attorney General 1913–15, Home Secretary 1915–16 and 1935–37, Foreign Secretary 1931–35, Chancellor of Exchequer 1937–40, Lord Chancellor 1940–45.

Henry Strauss, later Baron Conesford (1892–1974). Barrister. Conservative MP Norwich 1935–45, 1950–55, Combined English Universities 1946–50. Parliamentary Secretary Ministry Public Building and Works 1942–43, Ministry Town and Country Planning 1943–45, BoT 1951–55.

Sir Raymond Streat (1897–1979). Chairman of Manchester Cotton Board 1940–57.

Peter Thorneycroft, later Baron (1909–1994). Conservative MP Salford 1938–45, Monmouth 1945–66. Junior Minister 1945, President BoT 1951–57, Chancellor of the Exchequer 1957–58, Minister of Aviation 1960-62, Defence 1962–64, Chairman of Conservative Party Organization 1975–81.

Captain Charles Waterhouse (1893–1975). Conservative MP Leicester South 1924–45, Leicester SE 1950-57. Junior Lord of Treasury 1936, Comptroller of HM Household 1937–38, Treasurer 1938–39, Assistant Postmaster General 1939–41, Parliamentary Secretary BoT 1941–45.

G. L. Watkinson, later Sir Laurence (1896–1974). Civil servant. Principal Assistant Secretary (Industries & Manufactures) BoT, Under Secretary 1942–46, Deputy Secretary, Ministry Fuel & Power 1947–55.

Harold Wilson, later Baron Rievaulx (b 1916). University lecturer. Director of Economics and Statistics, Ministry of Fuel and Power 1943–44. Labour MP Ormskirk 1945–50, Huyton 1950–83. Parliamentary Secretary Ministry of Works 1945–47, Secretary for Overseas Trade 1947, President BoT 1947–51, Prime Minister 1964–70, 1974–76.

Sir Howard Kingsley Wood (1881–1943). Conservative MP Woolwich W 1918–43, Parliamentary Secretary Ministry of Health 1924–29, Board of Education 1931, Postmaster General 1931–35, Minister of Health 1935–38, Secretary of State for Air 1938–40, Lord Privy Seal 1940, Chancellor Exchequer 1940–43.

BIBLIOGRAPHY

Official histories of the Second World War

Central Statistical Office (CSO) (1951) *Statistical Digest of the War*, London: HMSO.
Hancock K. and Gowing M. (1949) *British War Economy*, London: HMSO.
Hargreaves J. and Gowing M. (1951) *Civil Industry and Trade*, London: HMSO.
Hurstfield J. (1953) *Control of Raw Materials*, London: HMSO.
Titmuss R. M. (1950) *Problems of Social Policy*, London: HMSO.

Other Government and Parliamentary Publications

– (1946) *Boots and Shoes: BoT Working Party Report*, London: HMSO.
(annual) *Clothing Quiz*, London: BoT/HMSO (in PRO, Imperial War Museum and elsewhere).
– (1941) *Concentration of Production*), London: HMSO (Cmnd 6258).
Box K. (1950) *Utility and the Public: report to the BoT* (unpublished).
Council for Art and Industry (1937) *Design and the Designer in Industry*, London: HMSO.
Council for Art and Industry (1945) *Report of the Dress Committee*, London: HMSO.
Foreman S. (1986) *Shoes and Ships and Sealing Wax: illustrated history of the Board of Trade 1776–1986*, London: HMSO.

Report of the Purchase Tax/Utility Committee (the 'Douglas' Committee)(1952), London: HMSO (Cmnd 8452).
HofC   *House of Commons Official Report* (Hansard).

Other published sources

Addison P. (1975) *The Road to 1945: British Politics and the Second World War*, London: Cape.
Addison P. (1985) *Now the War is Over*, London: BBC/Cape.
Addison P. (1992) *Churchill on the Home Front 1900–1955*, London: Cape.

Ady P. (1942) 'Utility Goods' in *Studies in War Economics*, Vol. 4, No. 15, Oxford: Blackwell.

Amies H. (1984) *Still Here*, London: Weidenfeld & Nicolson.

Barlow T. (1944) 'Conception, Birth and Development of Utility Fabrics', *Journal of Society of Dyers & Colourists*, March.

Barnett C. (1986) *Audit of War*, London: Macmillan.

Beardmore G. (1986) *Civilians at War*, Oxford: OUP.

Beaton C. (1954) *Glass of Fashion*, London: Weidenfeld & Nicolson.

Bernard J.-R. (1953) 'Le Système Utility', *Cahiers de la Fondation des Sciences Politiques* (46), Paris.

Bertram A. (1939) *Design*, London: Penguin.

Bradfield N. (1970) *Historical Costume of England 1066–1968*, London: Harrap.

Braithwaite B. et al. (1987) *The Home Front: the Best of Good Housekeeping 1939–1945*, London: Ebury Press.

Briggs A. (1984) *Marks & Spencer Ltd 1884–1984*, London: Octopus.

Briggs S. (1975) *Keep Smiling Through: Home Front 1939–1945*, London: Weidenfeld & Nicholson.

Broadberry S. (1988) 'Impact of World Wars on Long Run Performance of the British Economy', *Oxford Review of Economic Policy*, Spring.

Cairncross A. (1992) *British Economy since 1945*, Oxford: Blackwell.

Calder A. (1969) *The People's War*, London: Cape.

Calder A. (1991) *Myth of the Blitz*, London: Cape.

Calder A. and Sheridan D. (eds), (1985) *Speak for Yourself: a Mass-Observation Anthology 1937–49*, Oxford: OUP.

Carr-Saunders A. M. et al. (1958) *Survey of Social Conditions in England and Wales*, Oxford: OUP.

Chandos *see Lyttleton*.

Channon H. (1967) in Rhodes-James, R. (ed.), *Chips: Diaries of Sir Henry Channon*, London: Weidenfeld & Nicolson.

Chester D. (ed.) (1951) *Lessons of the British War Economy*, Cambridge: NIESR/CUP.

Cooke C. (1957) *Stafford Cripps*, London: Hodder & Stoughton.

Cunnington C. W. (1952) *English Women's Clothing in the Present Century*, London: Faber.

Dalton H. (1957) The Fateful Years 1931–1945, London: Muller.

Dalton H. (1986) in Pimlott B. (ed.), *Second World War Diaries*, London: Cape.

Docherty C. and Hann M. (1993) 'Stylistic Change in Womenswear Products; Part I: a Quantitative Analysis of Hem Length Variations

1946–1990', *Journal of the Textile Institute*, 84 (2).

Dorner J. (1975) Fashion in the Forties and Fifties, London: Ian Allan.

Dover H. (1991) *Home Front Furniture*, London: Scolar Press.

Ewing E. (1974) *History of 20th Century Fashion*, London: Batsford.

Forty A. (1980) *Objects of Desire: Design and Society 1750–1950*, London: Thames & Hudson.

Garland M. (1983) *History of Fashion*, London: Dent.

Harrison T. (ed.) (1961) *Britain Revisited*, London: Gollancz.

Harrison T. and Madge C. (1940) *War Begins at Home*, London: Chatto & Windus.

Hennessy P. (1992) *Never Again*, London: Cape.

Hillier B. (1975) *Austerity Binge*, London: Studio Vista.

Hobsbawm E. (1968) *Industry and Empire* (Pelican Economic History of Britain Vol. 3), London: Penguin.

Hopkins H. (1963) *The New Look: Social History of the 40s and 50s in Great Britain*, London: Secker & Warburg.

Idle D. (1944) *War Over West Ham*, London: Faber.

Jefferys J. (1954) *Retail Trading in Britain 1850–1950*, Cambridge: CUP.

Jenkins A. (1977) *The Forties*, London: Heinemann.

Laver J. (1979) *Concise History of Costume*, London: Thames & Hudson.

Lewis P. (1980) *The Fifties*, London: Herbert Press.

Longmate N. (1971) *How We Lived Then*, London: Hutchinson.

Lyttleton O. (Lord Chandos) (1962) *Memoirs*, London: Bodley Head.

Macarthy F. (1979) *History of British Design 1830–1970*, London: Allen & Unwin.

MacIver O. (1946) 'Family Life in Wartime', *Social Work* 3 (10), April.

Marquis F. *see* Woolton.

Marwick A. (1965) *The Deluge*, London: Bodley Head.

Marwick A. (1966) *Britain in the Century of Total War*, London: Bodley Head.

Niblett K. (1990) *Dynamic Design: the British Pottery Industry 1940–1990*, Stoke-on-Trent: Stoke City Museum.

Panter-Downes M. (1971) in W. Shawn (ed.) *London War Notes*, London: Longman.

Pelling H. (1970) *Britain and the Second World War*, London: Macmillan Press.

Philips P. (1963) 'The New Look' in M. Sissons and P. French (eds) *Age of Austerity*, Oxford: OUP.

Pimlott B. (1985) *Hugh Dalton*, London: Cape.

Pollard S. (1969) *Development of the British Economy 1914–1967*, London: Edward Arnold.

Rees G. (1973) *St Michael: History of Marks & Spencer*, London: Pan.

Ruby J. (1989) *Costume in Context: 1940s and 1950s*, London: Batsford.

Saunders E. (1954) *Age of Worth*, London: Longman Green.

Settle A. (1959) *English Fashion*, London: Collins.

Stevenson J. (1984) *British Society 1914–1945*, London: Penguin.

Swann J. (1982) *Shoes*, London: Batsford.

Taylor A. (1965) *English History 1914–1945*, Oxford: OUP.

Taylor A. (1975) *Second World War*, London: Putnam.

Vogue (1991) *Vogue 75 Years*, London: Condé Nast.

Wadsworth H. (1948) 'Utility Cloth and Clothing Scheme', *Review of Economic Studies*, XVI (2.40).

Walker J. (1989) *Design History and History of Design*, London: Pluto Press.

Woolton Lord (*Fred Marquis*) (1959) *Memoirs*, London: Cassell.

Worswick G. (1947) 'Concentration – success or failure?' in *Studies in War Economics*, Oxford: Oxford University Institute of Statistics/Blackwell.

Periodicals

Daily Mail
Daily Mirror
Drapers' Record (*now DR*)
Financial Times
News Chronicle
Picture Post
Sunday Chronicle
The Times

Unpublished Sources

(Abbreviations are those used in the text; complete references are given wherever appropriate)

BFMF   British Footwear Manufacturers Federation: minutes etc.

M-OA   Mass-Observation Archive, University of Sussex; file reports etc.

PRO   Public Record Office papers, from Board of Trade (BT), Cabinet Office (CAB), Central Office of Information (INF) and Treasury (T) classes.

Warwick Modern Records Centre, University of Warwick; TU and trade association papers.

INDEX